Core Blender Development

Understanding the Essential Source Code

Brad E. Hollister

Apress®

Core Blender Development: Understanding the Essential Source Code

Brad E. Hollister
Computer Science Department, CSUDH, Carson, CA, USA

ISBN-13 (pbk): 978-1-4842-6414-0   ISBN-13 (electronic): 978-1-4842-6415-7
https://doi.org/10.1007/978-1-4842-6415-7

Copyright © 2021 by Brad E. Hollister

Managing Director, Apress Media LLC: Welmoed Spahr
Acquisitions Editor: Natalie Pao
Development Editor: James Markham
Coordinating Editor: Jessica Vakili

Distributed to the book trade worldwide by Springer Science+Business Media New York, 1 NY Plaza, New York, NY 10014. Phone 1-800-SPRINGER, fax (201) 348-4505, e-mail orders-ny@springer-sbm.com, or visit www.springeronline.com. Apress Media, LLC is a California LLC and the sole member (owner) is Springer Science + Business Media Finance Inc (SSBM Finance Inc). SSBM Finance Inc is a **Delaware** corporation.

For information on translations, please e-mail booktranslations@springernature.com; for reprint, paperback, or audio rights, please e-mail bookpermissions@springernature.com.

Apress titles may be purchased in bulk for academic, corporate, or promotional use. eBook versions and licenses are also available for most titles. For more information, reference our Print and eBook Bulk Sales web page at http://www.apress.com/bulk-sales.

Any source code or other supplementary material referenced by the author in this book is available to readers on GitHub via the book's product page, located at www.apress.com/ 978-1-4842-6414-0. For more detailed information, please visit http://www.apress.com/ source-code.

Printed on acid-free paper

Table of Contents

About the Author

Brad E. Hollister holds a PhD from the University of California Santa Cruz in computer science. His research includes scientific visualization and virtual reality for training. Dr. Hollister is also faculty adviser for the Open-Source Mozilla Campus Club at the California State University Dominguez Hills.

CHAPTER 1

Intro to the "Core" Blender Source Code

The goal of this chapter is to familiarize you with the Blender "core" source[1], and is intended to be the starting point for the rest of the book. Blender's codebase is written primarily in the C programming language. Part of this introduction is a preliminary discussion of Blender's CMake build system. Additionally, we provide an execution trace of how Blender registers an operator, and of the execution of its callback. Much of this book will be easier to digest, if you make an effort to browse the source code in a text editor—ideally, after reading the associated passage. If you have not yet downloaded and compiled the Blender source code, you will eventually want to do so. However, this chapter may be read first.

The Blender Project

Throughout this book, we do not want to merely replicate the wealth of information already present at `https://developer.blender.org`. Nonetheless, we direct your attention to these valuable resources at the appropriate times. You should use those external documents in support of, and in tandem with, the material of this text.

---

[1]At the time of writing, version 2.90 was just released. The book was started while 2.83 was still current. However, the core principles of the Blender codebase have remained consistent over time. The book's code repository is based on the master branch Git revision (SHA1 ID) 28fca2c588fdfb44919ec82eddab19d8cf2e8c9e.

© Brad E. Hollister 2021
B. E. Hollister, *Core Blender Development*,
https://doi.org/10.1007/978-1-4842-6415-7_1

We endeavor to provide a separate perspective from the official guides. This book's goals are the following:

- To fill in "missing" parts of the Blender Foundation's documentation

- To present a simpler starting point in becoming a Blender "core" developer

- To go beyond existing documentation, so as to jump-start your efforts

Such experience could otherwise only be gained by direct inspection (and significant experimentation) of the source code. Ultimately, as you progress, that approach will be necessary as well.

Official Documentation

The official developer site is available at `https://developer.blender.org` (see Figure 1-1). There you will find the Blender Foundation's *Phabricator* site, responsible for being a portal to their code repositories, bug tracker, developer documents, etc.

Figure 1-1. *The Blender Foundation's portal for developers:* `https://developer.blender.org`

As aspects can change concerning how to clone and build Blender, and building is both platform specific and configurable, the best way to obtain up-to-date instructions is to visit `https://developer.blender.org`.

Communication Channels

It is helpful to speak with developers actively working on the core source code. While the Blender developer community maintains an Internet Relay Chat (IRC) room, located on Freenode in the channel **#blendercoders**, the latest way to interact in real-time is on `https://blender.chat`. **#blender-coders** is the relevant channel there, for developers (Figure 1-2).

Figure 1-2. Blender's browser-based chat server interface

As with most open source projects, Blender has an email list. This provides another key resource for communication with the Blender developer community. To post a message for "core" developers to read, and potentially answer, the email address is *bf-committers@blender.org* (see Figure 1-3). This is the appropriate list for developers (and, hopefully, eventually committers), as there are other mailing lists dedicated only to users, and other aspects of the Blender project apart from development.

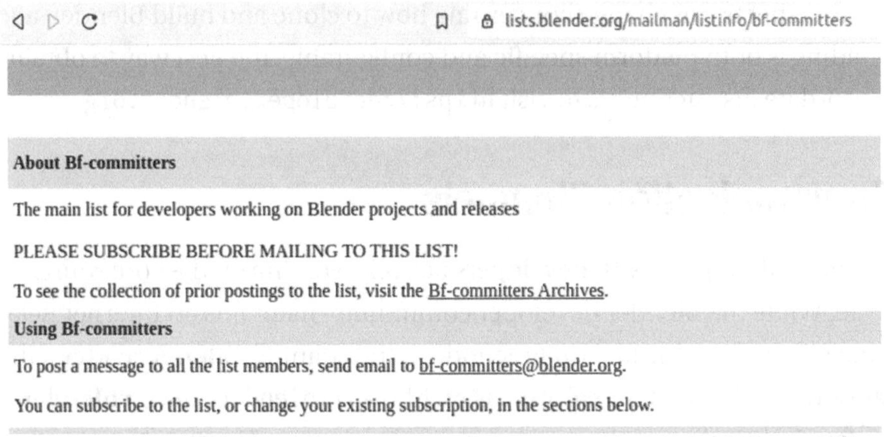

◁ ▷ C   🔖   🔒 lists.blender.org/mailman/listinfo/bf-committers

About Bf-committers

The main list for developers working on Blender projects and releases

PLEASE SUBSCRIBE BEFORE MAILING TO THIS LIST!

To see the collection of prior postings to the list, visit the Bf-committers Archives.

Using Bf-committers

To post a message to all the list members, send email to bf-committers@blender.org.

You can subscribe to the list, or change your existing subscription, in the sections below.

Figure 1-3. *Bf-committers subscription web page. This sign-up page is accessible from the official Blender project wiki*

The Blender Source Tree

To begin, you should become familiar with three essential documents. These are

- https://wiki.blender.org/wiki/Reference/ FAQ, which is unfortunately not found in the source distribution itself. It contains information on what Blender "DNA" and "RNA" are, along with the *datatoc* module.

- The second is the wiki description of the source code modules, https://wiki.blender.org/wiki/Source/ File_Structure.

- Third is the slightly out-of-date www.blender.org/bf/ codelayout.jpg. Inaccuracies are due to omission of newer modules.

There are other important documents that we will mention. But for starters, you should at least read the aforementioned material.

The key aspect of the *codelayout.jpg* information is the calling hierarchy of the modules. "Modules" in the Blender Project's parlance represent directories containing code related to a particular set of functions (much as a component is, in an object-oriented design). Some modules have interfaces for client modules. The Blender terminology for these interfaces is module "APIs."

The easiest way to begin browsing Blender's source is by using the project's repository server: `https://developer.blender.org/diffusion/B/`. There, you will also find the latest instructions on cloning the git repository.[2]

Start by looking at the top-level directory in the repository (Figure 1-4). The "core" Blender source code is in *source/* (Figure 1-5).

---

[2]If any of the URLs become broken, it is suggested to use `https://developer.blender.org` as a starting point to finding the source, etc. The primary developer site is likely to remain stable.

Figure 1-4. *The Eclipse IDE's "project explorer" view, from the CMake generated .proj. We can see that Blender contains many more directories than those of the "core" source code, located in source/. There is a directory for unit tests, that is, tests/. And, doc/ is for documentation. We will stay focused on source/, and go beyond it only when required*

Libraries not considered "core," but maintained by Blender, are in the *intern* directory. Notably, the ghost module is located there. We will, however, talk more about ghost (Generic Handy Operating System Toolkit) as it provides an abstraction to the underlying platform.

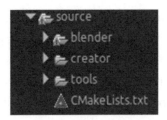

Figure 1-5. *The Eclipse IDE's "project explorer" view of source/.*
Note that in codelayout.jpg and `https://wiki.blender.org/wiki/`
`Source/File_Structure`*, this path would be written as blender/source/.*
Most of the official documents refer to the repository's directory as
blender/. However, during cloning with git, you can name this directory

Also in *intern* is an internal module called `guardedalloc`. This module
wraps the dynamic memory allocation functions from the C standard
library. The allocation functions are of the form:

```
MEM_[mc]allocN(unsigned int len, char * str)
```

Whenever Blender dynamically allocates (or deallocates) memory, you
will see the `MEM_*` API being used instead of `malloc`, `calloc`, etc. The `MEM_*`
API prototypes are available from *[Source Directory]/intern/guardedalloc/*
MEM_guardedalloc.h.

Note   The *[Source Directory]/doc/guides/* directory contains
additional official documentation on `guardedalloc` and the user
interface API. The two text files are *blender-guardedalloc.txt* and
interface_API.txt. We will talk more about the `UI_*` API in Chapter 8.
Much of the *interface_API.txt document is now obsolete, but still
contains useful information.*

There are modules that we will not concern ourselves with, due
to the scope of the codebase. Therefore, this book focuses on UI and

geometric modeling, along with the essential modules from Blender (e.g., windowmanager, blenloader, etc.). Figure 1-6 shows a listing of the "core" Blender modules.

For now, realize that modules serving as support for other modules have an *intern* subdirectory of their own. There will also be a number of header files above their *intern/*, which allow export (inclusion) of the interface function prototypes. For the module blenloader (Figure 1-7), we can see this convention in the source tree.

Figure 1-6. The "core" blender modules, showing the entire set located in source/blender/. The directory layout is split over two subfigures, left-to-right

In a general sense, the editors module is one of the highest in the module hierarchy, in that it only calls to lower-level functions. This module's contents (each subdirectory being an editor or tool, not to be confused with *source/tools*) ties together the support functionality of other modules. We will explore *editors/mesh/* (mesh operators or "tool" code), and *editors/space_view3d/* (an editor "view"), further in subsequent chapters.

Figure 1-7. *The* blenloader *module. The intern subdirectory contains the implementation of its interface and static "internal" functions. Blenloader's interface prototypes are located at the same level as intern/, in C header files. There is a similar layout for all modules with an API*

The Blender CMake Build System

Now let us discuss how Blender makes use of the CMake build system and how various modules can be included or excluded from a build.

The Basics

CMake is a "meta" build system, developed by Kitware. By "meta," it is implied that CMake acts as an abstraction layer over platform-specific build systems, such as autotools or Visual Studio. The official documentation for CMake is available at `https://cmake.org`. Kitware provides a complete description of their scripting language used to write *CMakeLists.txt* files there.

The responsibility of CMake is to produce build files for any given platform which is supported by Blender. CMake uses *CMakeLists.txt* files to direct the generation of platform-specific build scripts. For example, Blender's *CMakeLists.txt* files are written to support build script generation for Linux, Windows, and Mac OS, and for a chosen build script type on that platform, that is, Visual Studio vs. Makefile on Linux.

In Blender's source tree, a *CMakeLists.txt* file is provided at the top-level (shown in Figure 1-4) as the entry point. There is also a *CMakeLists. txt* file above the individual "core" modules (Figure 1-6) and in each of *blender/*, *creator/*, and *tools/* (Figure 1-5). There is at least one *CMakeLists. txt* file in every module directory (not necessarily one in a module's subdirectory, however) directing CMake to include the module's source files and headers. For instance, see the *CMakeLists.txt* file in Figure 1-7, for the *blenloader* module.

Listing 1-1 shows an excerpt from the entry-point *CMakeLists.txt*. In addition to setting various CMake built-in environment variables (e.g., CMAKE_BUILD_TYPE_INIT), new ones are defined (here, OpenGL_ GL_PREFERENCE, for instance). Also shown in Listing 1-1 is an inclusion of a number of modules (externally referenced CMake scripts), located at ${CMAKE_SOURCE_DIR}/build_files/cmake/Modules and ${CMAKE_ SOURCE_DIR}/build_files/cmake/platform.

Listing 1-1. Excerpt from the repository top-level CMakeLists.txt file[3]

```
...
cmake_minimum_required(VERSION 3.5)

# Prever LEGACY OpenGL to eb compatible with all the existing
releases and
# platforms which don't hare GLVND yet. Only do it if
preference was not set
# externally.
if(NOT DEFINED OpenGL_GL_PREFERENCE)
  set(OpenGL_GL_PREFERENCE "LEGACY")
endif()
```

---

[3]As this is the first listing in the book, note that each listing is verbatim from the distribution. At times, you will see typos and spelling errors, especially in the comments from the source. Here, we see that "hare" is a misspelling of "have." We do not mention any further typos in the source.

```
if(NOT EXECUTABLE_OUTPUT_PATH)
  set(FIRST_RUN TRUE)
else()
  set(FIRST_RUN FALSE)
endif()

# this starts out unset
list(APPEND CMAKE_MODULE_PATH "${CMAKE_SOURCE_DIR}/build_files/
cmake/Modules")
list(APPEND CMAKE_MODULE_PATH "${CMAKE_SOURCE_DIR}/build_files/
cmake/platform")

# avoid having empty buildtype
if(NOT DEFINED CMAKE_BUILD_TYPE_INIT)
  set(CMAKE_BUILD_TYPE_INIT "Release")
...
```

As this book is about "core" Blender development, we focus on the *CMakeLists.txt* files that direct the build system for the primary source code. You should verify that Blender's build system is more extensive than the *CMakeLists.txt* files in the repository's *source/* directory alone.

In Figure 1-8, we see the repository's *build_files/*, where "support" CMake modules for the "core" build system are located. Other types of build scripts (e.g., bash scripts or Python scripts) are also placed in *build_files/* for things such as downloading and building dependencies either for the development platform or internal and external libraries (e.g., the ones in *intern/* and *extern/* from Figure 1-4).

Figure 1-8. *The directories in the repository that comprise the build system. Most of the build system for "core" Blender is in the source/ directory, alongside the source files. We have CMake script support functions (defined in build_files/ subdirectories) or scripts for building Blender dependencies*

Module Build Options

CMake allows for exclusion of modules and their dependencies. Listing 1-2 has an excerpt from *source/blender/CMakeLists.txt*, showing modules that are included always in a build, and then the optional ones. The WITH_* variables are set by default in *source/CMakeLists.txt* and can be reconfigured after running the initial configuration with the cmake executable.

Listing 1-2. From source/blender/CMakeLists.txt, we see the "core" modules included by the add_subdirectory() CMake script function, along with conditional modules near the end of the snippet

...

```
add_subdirectory(datatoc)
add_subdirectory(editors)
add_subdirectory(windowmanager)
add_subdirectory(blenkernel)
```

```
add_subdirectory(blenlib)
add_subdirectory(bmesh)
add_subdirectory(draw)
add_subdirectory(render)
add_subdirectory(blenfont)
add_subdirectory(blentranslation)
add_subdirectory(blenloader)
add_subdirectory(depsgraph)
add_subdirectory(ikplugin)
add_subdirectory(physics)
add_subdirectory(gpu)
add_subdirectory(imbuf)
add_subdirectory(nodes)
add_subdirectory(modifiers)
add_subdirectory(gpencil_modifiers)
add_subdirectory(shader_fx)
add_subdirectory(makesdna)
add_subdirectory(makesrna)

if(WITH_COMPOSITOR)
  add_subdirectory(compositor)
endif()

if(WITH_IMAGE_OPENEXR)
  add_subdirectory(imbuf/intern/openexr)
endif()

if(WITH_OPENIMAGEIO)
  add_subdirectory(imbuf/intern/oiio)
endif()

if(WITH_IMAGE_DDS)
  add_subdirectory(imbuf/intern/dds)
endif()
```

```
if(WITH_IMAGE_CINEON)
  add_subdirectory(imbuf/intern/cineon)
endif()

if(WITH_CODEC_AVI)
  add_subdirectory(avi)
endif()

if(WITH_PYTHON)
  add_subdirectory(python)
endif()

if(WITH_OPENCOLLADA)
  add_subdirectory(collada)
endif()

if(WITH_FREESTYLE)
  add_subdirectory(freestyle)
endif()

if(WITH_ALEMBIC)
  add_subdirectory(alembic)
endif()
```

. . .

You should find it useful to reset some of these options when configuring your build. Beyond what is shown here, there are more fine-grained configurations for builds. CMake actually defines C preprocessor macros to allow inclusion of individual lines of source code, instead of the coarser-level "whole" directories we show in Listing 1-2.

It is advisable that when building Blender for the first time, that you build in debug mode, by setting CMAKE_BUILD_TYPE_INIT to "Debug." This can be done through the cmake executable after the initial configuration, or by changing the *source/CMakeLists.txt* file itself.

A Representative Code Example

Let us commence with exploring the Blender code, by a concrete example. It will relate UI interaction with the operator code tied to particular UI events. The purpose of this relatively simple example is to lay some groundwork for more future descriptions about operators and related topics.

Geometric Modeling and Operators

We wish to get the "ball rolling," as it were, by introducing operator registration and associated callback invocation. Thus, we will trace the execution path taken by Blender when a user creates a spherical model, regarding the operator registration for that case.

Operators in Blender are essentially functions (and state) that are called when they are triggered by the UI. They are more than just a callback in Blender. We will mostly focus on the callback portion, in our example trace.

First, let us investigate operator registration. As we are interested in creating a sphere primitive, an icosphere modeled with polygons, we note the registration of this operator via MESH_OT_primitive_ico_sphere_ add(). This function is defined in *source/blender/editors/mesh/editmesh_ add.c*.

The actual registration entails the *windowmanager*'s WM_ operatortype_append() and wmOperatorType struct. We will eventually describe these items more specifically further along in the book, together with naming conventions for module APIs. Relevant now is ED_ operatortypes_mesh(), shown in Figure 1-9 and Listing 1-3.

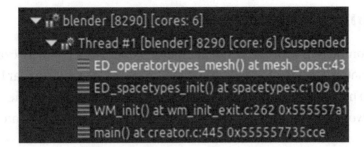

Figure 1-9. *During Blender initialization, mesh operators are registered. The windowmanager module is called from* main()*, located in source/creator/creator.c, which subsequently calls the editor module's* ED_operatortypes_mesh()*. The call stack is shown here (from gdb within the Eclipse IDE). Hexadecimal numbers are the logical addresses of the functions. These numbers are unimportant here, and sometimes may be partially abbreviated for clarity*

Figure 1-9 exhibits the call stack at the point when ED_operatortypes_ mesh() is executed. This is part of the regular initialization of Blender. We started in main() from source/creator/*creator.c*, and then there is a cascade of calls from the windowmanager module to the editor module, first starting from WM_init()—that is, the high-level windowmanager initialization routine. We see in Listing 1-3 a snippet of ED_operatortypes_ mesh().

Listing 1-3. Excerpt from ED_operatortypes_mesh() from source/ blender/editors/mesh/mesh_ops.c. This code snippet shows operator registration for many of the "primitives" that can be easily created by either menu or hotkey combinations. MESH_OT_ primitive_ico_sphere_add is a function pointer and is in bold type

```
/*************************** registration *******************
*************/
```

```
void ED_operatortypes_mesh(void)
{
  ...
  WM_operatortype_append(MESH_OT_primitive_cone_add);
  WM_operatortype_append(MESH_OT_primitive_grid_add);
  WM_operatortype_append(
               MESH_OT_primitive_monkey_add);
  WM_operatortype_append(
               MESH_OT_primitive_uv_sphere_add);
  WM_operatortype_append(
               MESH_OT_primitive_ico_sphere_add);
  ...
```

The call to `WM_operatortype_append()` connects the operator to the Blender "RNA" system (Listing 1-4). We defer a discussion about Blender "RNA" until the appropriate chapter, but `wm_operatortype_append__begin()` from *source/blender/windowmanager/intern/wm_operator_type.c* forms part of this "gluing" process.

Listing 1-4. The `WM_operatortype_append()` function. This function calls `MESH_OT_primitive_ico_sphere_add()` to register the operator shown in bold type

```
/* all ops in 1 list (for time being... needs evaluation later) */
void WM_operatortype_append(void (*opfunc)(wmOperatorType *))
{
  wmOperatorType *ot =
         wm_operatortype_append__begin();
  opfunc(ot);
  wm_operatortype_append__end(ot);
}
```

Also in WM_operatortype_append(), we call MESH_OT_primitive_ico_ sphere_add(). MESH_OT_primitive_sphere_add() is shown in Listing 1-5. Notice the wmOperatorType object (referenced by ot) has an exec field. MESH_OT_primitive_ico_sphere_add() assigns the callback add_ primitive_icosphere_exec() to the wmOperatorType object's exec field. There are also other aspects of the operator registration, like setting the name, description, id name, and other fields of the wmOperatorType struct.

Listing 1-5. MEST_OT_primitive_ico_sphere_add(), an operator registration function from source/blender/editors/mesh/editmesh_ add.c. Setting the callback for the operator is in bold type

```
void MESH_OT_primitive_ico_sphere_add(wmOperatorType *ot)
{
  /* identifiers */
  ot->name = "Add Ico Sphere";
  ot->description = "Construct an Icosphere mesh";
  ot->idname = "MESH_OT_primitive_ico_sphere_add";

  /* api callbacks */
  ot->exec = add_primitive_icosphere_exec;
  ot->poll = ED_operator_scene_editable;

  /* flags */
  ot->flag = OPTYPE_REGISTER | OPTYPE_UNDO;

  /* props */
  RNA_def_int(ot->srna, "subdivisions", 2, 1, 10,
  "Subdivisions", "", 1, 8);

  ED_object_add_unit_props_radius(ot);
  ED_object_add_mesh_props(ot);
  ED_object_add_generic_props(ot, true);
}
```

Listing 1-6 shows the add_primitive_icosphere_exec() callback implementation, defined in the same source file as MESH_OT_primitive_ ico_sphere_add(). It is declared static, so that only the callback mechanism (operator) has access to the function.

Listing 1-6. Elided add_primitive_icosphere_exec() callback function, from source/blender/editors/mesh/editmesh_add.c. Notice the bContext struct pointer called C, and the call to the makesrna module via RNA_boolean_get(). These are important parts of the Blender architecture, for maintaining and conveying state information

```
static int add_primitive_icosphere_exec(bContext *C,
wmOperator *op)
{
  MakePrimitiveData creation_data;
  Object *obedit;
  BMEditMesh *em;
  float loc[3], rot[3];
  bool enter_editmode;
  ushort local_view_bits;
  const bool calc_uvs = RNA_boolean_get(op->ptr, "calc_uvs");

  WM_operator_view3d_unit_defaults(C, op);
  ED_object_add_generic_get_opts(C, op, 'Z', loc, rot, &enter_
  editmode, &local_view_bits, NULL);
  obedit = make_prim_init(C,
                          CTX_DATA_(BLT_I18NCONTEXT_ID_MESH,
                          "Icosphere"),
                          loc,
                          rot,
                          local_view_bits,
                          &creation_data);
```

```
em = BKE_editmesh_from_object(obedit);

...


return OPERATOR_FINISHED;
}
```

If a user creates an icosphere from the UI, add_primitive_icosphere_exec() will be called in response. Figure 1-10 shows the call stack for this scenario.

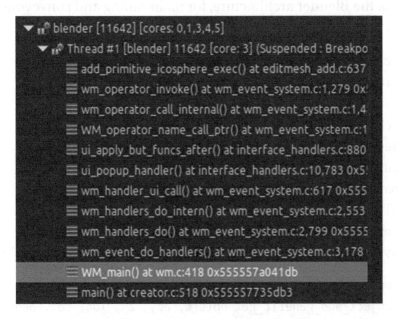

Figure 1-10. WM_main() *is the event loop for Blender, located in source/blender/windowmanager/intern/wm.c.* wm_event_do_handlers() *is the high-level function updating the callback (or handler) mechanism. We see here that* add_primitive_icosphere_exec() *is called after having been registered, and now invoked from the UI*

We will not go further into add_primitive_icosphere_exec(), as the point of this example is to illustrate operator registration and invocation of a callback (other operators are registered similarly). For the present, however, notice the interaction with the module makesrna and the bContext struct called C (Listing 1-6). The global variable named C is significant.

Blender's Event Loop

WM_main() contains the event loop for Blender, as shown in Listing 1-7. C, the same object of type bContext struct as already mentioned, is passed to each of the high-level update function calls of the event loop. All of these are wrappers who either collect events, process callbacks based on those events, or broadcast notifiers based on event processing.

The last routine in the event loop to execute is wm_draw_update(). Once all model data is updated, then the view is updated. Blender is a Model-View-Controller (MVC) application, and as such, the "model" parts are updated first, and then the "view."

Listing 1-7. Blender's main event loop, called WM_main(), is defined in source/blender/windowmanager/intern/wm.c

```
void WM_main(bContext *C)
{
  /* Single refresh before handling events.
   * This ensures we don't run operators before the depsgraph
   has been evaluated. */
  wm_event_do_refresh_wm_and_depsgraph(C);
```

```
while (1) {

    /* get events from ghost, handle window events, add to
    window queues */
    wm_window_process_events(C);

    /* per window, all events to the window, screen, area and
    region handlers */
    wm_event_do_handlers(C);

    /* events have left notes about changes, we handle and
    cache it */
    wm_event_do_notifiers(C);

    /* execute cached changes draw */
    wm_draw_update(C);
  }
}
```

Note   The preceding trace was shown using the call stack and code snippets of the relevant execution path. If you are a visual learner, you will find it beneficial to use Doxygen.[4] A sample call graph is shown in Figure 1-11. Because these call graphs are often very large, the proper way to display them is interactively from html. We will discuss Doxygen again in a later chapter.

---

[4]www.doxygen.nl/manual/diagrams.html.

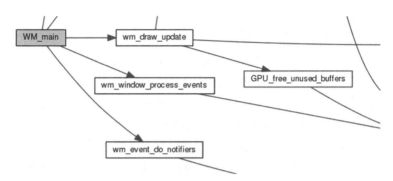

Figure 1-11. *Partial view of* WM_main() *'s call graph. Such call graphs are easily generated using Doxygen*

Road Map for the Remainder of the Book

In this first chapter, we went over some of the basics of the Blender code. We made a distinction between "core" Blender and the other parts of the codebase. We showed how a build of Blender is managed by CMake and how CMake can generate build scripts for various platforms. We also talked a little about operators and callbacks and saw how they worked in the creation of an icosphere.

What Will Not Be Covered

As the Blender codebase is vast, we will not cover things like the game engine and the rendering subsystems (e.g., "Blender Internal," or Cycles). We will also not describe "core" code related to physics, compositing, animation, or modifiers. Nor will we extensively discuss the full set of editors, such as the outliner, etc.

What Will Be Covered

Going forward, we will break down a series of central "core" modules. We will discuss Blender's "DNA," the underlying records that maintain the state for Blender. We will also discuss how Blender integrates its embedded Python interpreter, how its UI is constructed at the C code level, and how Blender's "RNA" is related to all of this. We will walk through the C code that draws the UI, an OpenGL-based set of widgets internal to Blender itself (and therefore, "core" Blender). The `windowmanager` module will be analyzed, as it is the primary module of Blender. And, we will decompose polygonal mesh operators to a low level and show how the corresponding mesh data structures are managed. Finally, we will create a new editor within the `editor` module, using C code to do so.

The focus of this text is how Blender's code works as an application and how it processes aspects of polygonal models, namely, the basic polygonal mesh editor operations. Knowing this information should eventually allow developers to investigate areas of the Blender codebase beyond the material of this text.

## CHAPTER 2

Blender "DNA" and Serialization

This chapter explains Blender's persistent data model and related data structures. We first discuss a high-level description of the blend file. One of the most interesting aspects about the blend file is that it has been engineered to be very fast. Its contents are a binary image of memory, when the file was serialized. Blender supports backward compatibility, making the required transformations of the data structures in a given release to any later release. We will discuss the mechanics of reading a blend file. Because the blend file is a direct copy of runtime data structures, a good understanding of the blend file will support our understanding of how Blender maintains state and manages scene contents, such as objects and mesh data.

Blend File Overview

What Does the Blend File Contain?

The blend file consists of file-blocks that store the in-memory bytes for every C-style struct object (for a particular version of Blender) when the state of a Blender instance is serialized. These C-style structs are more commonly referred to as Blender's "DNA." The blend file also provides a

B. E. Hollister, *Core Blender Development*,
https://doi.org/10.1007/978-1-4842-6415-7_2

version's "DNA" struct definitions called SDNA and information on pointer-size and big- vs. little-endian byte order on the host machine that originally saved the file.

In this book, we do not show the header and file-block layout of the blend file, as this is documented by Joroen Bakker's "The Mystery of the Blend: The Blender File-Format Explained." His description along with two Python scripts, one for reading blend files and another for exporting the SDNA information, is in the Blender repository. Each file is located at *doc/blender_file_format/*.

mystery_of_the_blend.html, while written when Blender 2.54 was current, is still relevant. The "DNA" system employed by Blender has not changed, although the layout and addition of new structures have been made since the 2.54 release. The blend file is self-descriptive. It contains meta-data to interpret the file-block byte-level data, via both a dedicated file-block on the field data of the "DNA" structs (called "DNA1") and the file header—again, both discussed thoroughly in *mystery_of_the_blend. html*.

Using the BlendFileReader.py Script

What might be unclear from *mystery_of_the_blend.html* is how the two included Python scripts, *BlendFileReader.py* and *BlendFileDnaExporter_25. py*, operate. In fact, *BlendFileDnaExporter_25.py* is a misnomer and works for subsequent versions as well. It utilizes *BlendFileReader.py*. By invoking an executable of Blender to save a blend file, *BlendFileDnaExporter_25. py* reads the generated blend file's SDNA information. From the "DNA1" file-block, this script outputs html to display hyperlinked tables with the "DNA" struct fields from the generated blend file (excerpt shown in Figure 2-1).

Blender 2.83.5
Internal SDNA structures

Architecture: 64 bit Little endianness
Build revision: b'28fca2c588fd'
File format reference: The mystery of the blend by Jeroen Bakker

Index of blender structures

(0) Link	(1) LinkData	(2) ListBase
(3) vec2s	(4) vec2f	(5) vec3f
(6) rcti	(7) rctf	(8) DualQuat
(9) DrawDataList	(10) IDPropertyData	(11) IDProperty
(12) IDOverrideLibraryPropertyOperation	(13) IDOverrideLibraryProperty	(14) IDOverrideLibrary
(15) ID	(16) Library
(17) PreviewImage	(18) IpoDriver	(19) IpoCurve
(20) Ipo	(21) KeyBlock	(22) Key

Figure 2-1. *Excerpt from the beginning of the BlendFileDnaExporter_25.py output. The title states these are "SDNA structures," but possibly more accurate is that they are the "DNA" type struct field information read from the SDNA blocks, included in the "DNA1" file-block of the blend file. There is a separate SDNA* struct, *which is itself a "DNA" type* struct

Actually, using *BlenderFileDnaExporter_25.py* is not necessary, unless one wants an html representation of the DNA. It also only reads the SDNA file-block. We should really inspect the source code in the *makesdna* module for the "DNA" struct definitions, as this is the preferable route for a Blender developer. Also, by only using *BlenderFileDnaExporter_25.py*, we do not get a full description of how to use *BlendFileReader.py's* interface. Therefore, we will cover *makesdna* in terms of where the DNA structs are defined.

First, we will discuss how *BlendFileReader.py* ingests blend files, to better appreciate the blend file itself. *BlendFileReader.py* contains the openBlendFile() function that returns a Python file object, allowing a client program to create an instance of *BlendFileReader.py*'s BlendFile class definition. The openBlendFile() function checks whether the blend file contains the "BLENDER" string in its header. If not, it proceeds to try to decompress the file, if it is gzipped. Assuming that the file is valid and uncompressed, openBlendFile() returns the file object corresponding to the blend file.

After a client program receives the file object, it should pass it to the BlendFile constructor. BlendFile's __init__() method creates a list to contain the headers of each of the blend file-blocks, along with a member variable to hold the blend file header information. It loops over all of the blend file-blocks and stores self.Catalog (an instance of *BlendFileReader. py*'s DNACatalog) from the "DNA1" file-block, that is, the "DNA" struct fields. Incidentally, there are a few utility functions that the classes in BlendFile use for low-level file operations, such as seeking and byte alignment. The DNACatalog definition from *BlenderReader.py* is shown in Listing 2-1.

Listing 2-1. DNACatalog definition from BlenderReader.py

```
class DNACatalog:
    '''

    DNACatalog is a catalog of all information in the DNA1
    file-block

    Header = None
    Names = None
    Types = None
    Structs = None
    '''

    def __init__(self, fileheader, handle):
        log.debug("building DNA catalog")
        self.Names = []
        self.Types = []
        self.Structs = []
        self.Header = fileheader
```

```python
SDNA = ReadString(handle, 4)

# names
NAME = ReadString(handle, 4)
numberOfNames = Read('uint', handle, fileheader)
log.debug("building #{0} names".format(numberOfNames))
for i in range(numberOfNames):
    name = ReadString(handle, 0)
    self.Names.append(DNAName(name))
Align(handle)

# types
TYPE = ReadString(handle, 4)
numberOfTypes = Read('uint', handle, fileheader)
log.debug("building #{0} types".format(numberOfTypes))
for i in range(numberOfTypes):
    type = ReadString(handle, 0)
    self.Types.append(DNAType(type))
Align(handle)

# type lengths
TLEN = ReadString(handle, 4)
log.debug("building #{0} type-lengths".\
    format(numberOfTypes))
for i in range(numberOfTypes):
    length = Read('ushort', handle, fileheader)
    self.Types[i].Size = length
Align(handle)

# structs
STRC = ReadString(handle, 4)
numberOfStructures = Read('uint', handle, fileheader)
log.debug("building #{0} structures".\
    format(numberOfStructures))
```

```
for structureIndex in range(numberOfStructures):
    type = Read('ushort', handle, fileheader)
    Type = self.Types[type]
    structure = DNAStructure(Type)
    self.Structs.append(structure)

    numberOfFields = Read('ushort', handle, fileheader)
    for fieldIndex in range(numberOfFields):
        fTypeIndex = Read('ushort', handle, fileheader)
        fNameIndex = Read('ushort', handle, fileheader)
        fType = self.Types[fTypeIndex]
        fName = self.Names[fNameIndex]
```

Each blend file high-level construct creates instances of lower-level constructs in *BlendFileReader.py*. At the DNACatalog level, it creates copies of "NAMES," "TYPES," "TLEN," and "STRC" (the "DNA1" file-block data sections) using the corresponding classes: DNAName, DNAType, and DNAStructure. "TLEN" is the exception, as it represents a field of the DNAType called Size.

An example use of *BlendFileReader.py* is given in Listing 2-2. This sample displays the "holistic" information from the blend file header: (1) number of file-blocks and (2) the number of names, types, and structs in the "DNA1" file-block.

Listing 2-2. Example use of BlendFileReader.py. Client code reads the blend header and searches for a file-block. This is performed on the repository's file copy of startup.blend

```
import BlendFileReader as bfr

BLENDFILE = '../../release/datafiles/startup.blend' # pwd is
where BlendFileReader.py is in the repo
decomp_handle = bfr.openBlendFile(BLENDFILE)
startup = bfr.BlendFile(decomp_handle)
```

```
print('# of Blocks in startup: {}'.format(len(startup.Blocks)))
print('# of Names in startup SDNA: {}'.format(len(startup.
Catalog.Names)))
print('# of Types in startup SDNA: {}'.format(len(startup.
Catalog.Types)))
print('# of Structs in startup SDNA: {}'.format(len(startup.
Catalog.Structs)))

for blocknum, block in enumerate(startup.Blocks):
    sdna_idx = block.Header.SDNAIndex
    dna_type = startup.Catalog.Structs[sdna_idx].Type.Name
    #print(dna_type)
    if dna_type == 'Material':
        print('Block {}\n\tHeader code: {}'.format(blocknum,\
                        block.Header.Code))
        print('\tSNDA index: {}'.format(sdna_idx))
        print('\tType name: {}'.format(dna_type))
        print('\tOld address: {}'.\
            format(startup.Blocks[blocknum].Header.
            OldAddress))
```

The client code from Listing 2-2 also enumerates and searches for all instances of the Material "DNA" type from the file-blocks stored in the BlendFile instance.

A Closer Look at the makesdna Module

The *makedna* module in Blender provides definitions for state in Blender. It does this with a number of header files in *source/blender/makesdna/*. The first few listed in alphabetical order are *DNA_action_types.h*, *DNA_anim_types.h*, and *DNA_armature_types.h*. This module also includes an SDNA struct definition (defined in *DNA_sdna_types.h*), which outlines the version record of all other structs defined in the *makesdna* module. This SDNA `struct` is also used to represent the SDNA information read from a blend file.

Defaults for the "DNA" structs are provided in *source/blender/makesdna/*, and each called *DNA_*_defaults.h*, for every *DNA_*_types.h*. Not all DNA types are given defaults, however. The source file *source/blender/makesdna/intern/dna_defaults.c* contains macros that expand to definitions of struct objects named respectively, DNA_DEFAULT_##struct_name, for each of the DNA types that have default definitions. These default DNA type objects are assigned to the array entries of the defaults table called DNA_default_table[].

To serialize a blend file, Blender writes to a file a variable called DNAStr. DNAStr is a char array, which is the "DNA1" file-block of a blend file. DNAStr is defined in a file named *dna.c* and located in the *makesdna* mirrored directory of the source repository. In other words, *dna.c* is deposited within the build directory of the same name and relative path. The source file *dna.c* is not part of the repository source. It is generated from the executable *makesdna*, compiled and ran during the Blender build process from the file *source/blender/makesdna/intern/makesdna.c*. The *makesdna* executable picks up the Blender version's "DNA" types from the headers in the *makesdna* module, already described.

The remaining source files in *source/blender/makesdna/intern/* are *dna_genfile.c, dna_rename_defs.h, dna_utils.c,* and *dna_utils.h*. The header *dna_rename_defs.h* is interesting, in that the redefinition macros written there are expanded for the macro definition from the DNA_alias_maps() implementation, defined in *dna_utils.c* (see Listing 2-3). Conversions are made in the macro expansions for older fields and "DNA" `struct` names. These are added to hash maps for lookup during blend file loading of prior versions of the Blender executable.

Listing 2-3. Expansion of the redefinition macros defined in dna_
rename_defs.h in DNA_alias_maps() from dna_utils.c (in bold type).
DNA_alias_maps() is abbreviated here

```
void DNA_alias_maps(enum eDNA_RenameDir version_dir, GHash
**r_struct_map, GHash **r_elem_map)
{
  GHash *struct_map_local = NULL;
  if (r_struct_map) {
    const char *data[][2] = {
      #define DNA_STRUCT_RENAME(old, new) {#old, #new},
      #define DNA_STRUCT_RENAME_ELEM(struct_name, old, new)
      #include "dna_rename_defs.h"
      #undef DNA_STRUCT_RENAME
      #undef DNA_STRUCT_RENAME_ELEM
    };

  ...

  if (r_elem_map != NULL) {
    const char *data[][3] = {
      #define DNA_STRUCT_RENAME(old, new)
      #define DNA_STRUCT_RENAME_ELEM(struct_name, old, new)
      {#struct_name, #old, #new},
      #include "dna_rename_defs.h"
      #undef DNA_STRUCT_RENAME
      #undef DNA_STRUCT_RENAME_ELEM
    };
      ...
```

The internal API for the *makesdna* module is largely provided by the
extern functions defined in *dna_genfile.c*, while others are present in *dna_
utils.c*. Module APIs, as will be discussed in a side note later in this chapter,

are extern functions available to code from other modules within Blender and usually prefaced with a three capital letter abbreviation of the module. In the case of *makesdna*, this is DNA_*.

The file *dna_genfile.c* provides functions for creating and accessing a SDNA struct, along with writing the "DNA1" file-block to a blend file. The *dna_utils.c* file provides low-level API functions. One such function provides the size of a two-dimensional array from a char array read from a blend file. Other functions from *dna_utils.c* provide string processing routines associated with both writing and reading the blend file. The source file *dna_genfile.c* will be explored again in the next section, in the context of the execution path for the default loading of the *startup.blend* file.

Blend File Loading Trace in Core Blender: A First Encounter

The following explanation is meant as a first step in understanding the code in Blender that handles blend file reading and to provide a reference point for deeper inquiry. As such, you are encouraged to read the source for data structures and function definitions that are mentioned here only in passing, as the scale of the code is not possible to explain in full detail.

After having covered some of the fundamentals of the blend file, let us consider how Blender first encounters a *startup.blend* file during initialization. Code execution for the Blender executable begins in *source/creator/creator.c*, at the function main(). We now focus on the execution path that loads the *startup.blend* file.

The struct bContext and struct Main Types

Before we can appreciate this process, there are a couple of core Blender concepts to understand. First, the top-level data structure for maintaining Blender's state is a struct named struct bContext. Look at the bContext struct in Listing 2-4. It is defined, appropriately, in *source/blender/blenkernel/intern/context.c.*

Listing 2-4. The `struct bContext` definition. The `struct Main` data member is in bold type for emphasis

```
struct bContext {
  int thread;

  /* windowmanager context */
  struct {
    struct wmWindowManager *manager;
    struct wmWindow *window;
    struct WorkSpace *workspace;
    struct bScreen *screen;
    struct ScrArea *area;
    struct ARegion *region;
    struct ARegion *menu;
    struct wmGizmoGroup *gizmo_group;
    struct bContextStore *store;
    const char *operator_poll_msg; /* reason for poll failing */
  } wm;

  /* data context */
  struct {
    struct Main *main;
    struct Scene *scene;

    int recursion;
    /** True if python is initialized. */
    bool py_init;
    void *py_context;
  } data;
};
```

This `struct` contains two additional struct variables (`wm` and `data`), each with their own pointers to data structures describing UI (user-interface) elements and scene contents, respectively. In this text, the UI are of primary concern.

Note   Because *creator.c* includes the header, *source/blender/ blenkernel/BKE_context.h*, `struct bContext` is forward-declared. It is often the case that structs used throughout Blender's source are defined in a header file, above a module's "intern" subdirectory. The origination of the `struct bContext` definition inside a source file, contained in `blenkernel`'s intern subdirectory, communicates meaningful semantics and encapsulation. `struct bContext` should only be operated on through the accessor functions within the *context.c* source file. Most of *context.c*'s functions have external linkage, while only helper utilities for those accessor functions are declared with static linkage (and thus inaccessible outside of *context.c*).

Almost every aspect of the bContext `struct` is stored in the blend file—with the exception of the last three members of both `wm` and `data`. We will address `wm` in a later chapter. For now, let us discuss `struct data`. The `data struct` in `struct bContext` holds two other sub-structs: one of the `struct Main` type and another of `struct Scene`. The `struct Main` is defined in *source/blender/blenkernel/BKE_main.h*, whereas the `struct Scene` is defined in *source/blender/makesdna/DNA_scene_types.h*.

While there is a vast amount of state stored in both of these data types, it is perhaps more instructive to consider only parts of these records with the most obvious information first. Broadly, scene objects are contained in `struct Main`, but information related to the scene view is stored in struct Scene (which further uses struct Camera and struct World to encapsulate data, i.e., both of these structs contain physics, audio, and background color settings).

As we are working our way toward understanding geometric modeling (and later UI), we will continue to explore parts of struct Main. The struct Main member is a storehouse of Blender objects, and most of the file-block types encountered in the blend file layout are binary images of the "DNA" structs stored in struct Main's linked-lists.

There are a number of linked-lists (Listing 2-5) in struct Main. Each is headed by a ListBase struct (defined in *source/blender/makesdna/ DNA_listBase.h*, which simply contains first and last void pointers of the list nodes) and named after their content. These field declarations come after Blender version information, and pointers to other potentially stored struct Main instances linked from the Main struct object stored in the singleton struct bContext.

Listing 2-5. Linked-lists declared in the struct Main definition

```
    ListBase scenes;
  ListBase libraries;
  ListBase objects;
  ListBase meshes;
  ListBase curves;
  ListBase metaballs;
  ListBase materials;
  ListBase textures;
  ListBase images;
  ListBase lattices;
  ListBase lights;
  ListBase cameras;
  ListBase ipo; /* Deprecated (only for versioning). */
  ListBase shapekeys;
```

```
ListBase worlds;
ListBase screens;
ListBase fonts;
ListBase texts;
ListBase speakers;
ListBase lightprobes;
ListBase sounds;
ListBase collections;
ListBase armatures;
ListBase actions;
ListBase nodetrees;
ListBase brushes;
ListBase particles;
ListBase palettes;
ListBase paintcurves;
ListBase wm; /* Singleton (exception). */
ListBase gpencils;
ListBase movieclips;
ListBase masks;
ListBase linestyles;
```

Initialization of SDNA, Global, and the windowmanager

In *source/creator/creator.c*'s main(), there are many calls to initialize various parts of the application. The first call directly related to the Blender's DNA types is DNA_sdna_current_init(), defined in *source/blender/makesdna/intern/dna_genfile.c*. This function assigns an SDNA struct object to a global static variable called g_sdna. The g_sdna variable is accessible via the extern accessor functions of *dna_genfile.c*.

> **Note**   Most of the structs in the Blender source are `typedef`'ed
> with an identifier. There does not appear to be a reason why
> structs such as SDNA use this convention, whereas others, like
> `struct bContext`, do not. One can speculate this is a result of
> the preferences of the original authors or that a record like SDNA is
> meant to store data about other structs, and thus type-defining SDNA
> makes the singleton SDNA declaration a more clear abstraction.

SDNA (see Listing 2-6) is a meta-record, providing information about all
of the potential serializable data for the version of Blender that is running.
This `struct` is defined in *source/blender/makesdna/DNA_sdna_types.h*. It
is the same SDNA that is written into a blend file.

Listing 2-6. The SDNA record. Parts of SDNA related to hashing and
aliases are removed for clarity

```
typedef struct SDNA {
  /** Full copy of 'encoded' data (when data_alloc is set,
  otherwise borrowed). */
  const char *data;
  /** Length of data. */
  int data_len;
  bool data_alloc;

  /** Total number of struct members. */
  int names_len, names_len_alloc;
  /** Struct member names. */
  const char **names;
  /** Result of #DNA_elem_array_size (aligned with #names). */
  short *names_array_len;
```

```
    /** Size of a pointer in bytes. */
    int pointer_size;

    /** Type names. */
    const char **types;
    /** Number of basic types + struct types. */
    int types_len;

    /** Type lengths. */
    short *types_size;
/**
    * sp = structs[a] is the address of a struct definition
    * sp[0] is struct type number, sp[1] amount of members
    *
    * (sp[2], sp[3]), (sp[4], sp[5]), .. are the member
    * type and name numbers respectively.
    */
    short **structs;
    /** Number of struct types. */
    int structs_len;

...

} SDNA;
```

After having created an instance of the singleton SDNA object, we return back to main() and subsequently call BKE_blender_globals_init(). Another global struct, of type Global, is allocated a block of memory, the size of struct Main, and assigned to a pointer called main in Global. The allocation is performed by Blender's memory allocation module *source/intern/memutil*, wrapping C library functions for memory management. This will be the struct Main to be filled out by reading either the char array of bytes representing the in-memory *startup.blend* for a "factory startup" or from a serialized binary data file (arbitrary blend file).

There is another executable binary called *datatoc*, not to be confused with the module *datatoc*, that outputs the source file *startup.blend.c*. The *startup.blend.c* file is generated at build time and therefore deposited in the build directory. Within *startup.blend.c* is a char array with the "factory" *startup.blend* file contents. The char array is called `datatoc_startup_blend`. We will continue to track the path of execution until the point where our "factory startup" execution path encounters `datatoc_startup_blend`.

After `BKE_blender_globals_init()` is called, there are a number of initializations that occur. These are responsible for parsing command arguments and starting various subsystems such as sound, image buffers, materials, etc. None of these routines load state from the *startup.blend* file. Loading does not happen until we reach `WM_init()`. The `windowmanager` module is passed our `struct bContext`-type variable called `C`, where it will receive its `data` member information (recall that `struct bContext.data` is a struct composed of pointers to a `struct Main` and `struct Scene` object).

Upon entering `WM_init()`, there are initializations, many of which set callback functions for the *windowmanager* module. All of these occur before blend file loading. It is not until the call to `wm_homefile_read()` that we begin executing code to read *startup.blend*.

Realize that `wm_homefile_read()` is also called from two operator callbacks registered with the *windowmanager*, namely, `WM_OT_read_homefile()` and `WM_OT_read_userpref()`. However, we are not concerned with those paths of execution. Both are invoked via Blender's graphical user interface after initialization. `WM_init()` takes care of calling `wm_homefile_read()` with the correct parameters for a "factory startup," which is to read from the in-memory copy (`datatoc_startup_blend`) of the standard *startup.blend* file.

From the Kernel to the Loader

While `wm_homefile_read()` has conditions to handle parameters that require application templates that differ from factory settings, our journey through wm_homefile_read() settles on BKE_blendfile_read_from_memory() (see Listing 2-7), given the parameters set in WM_init().

Listing 2-7. Calling BKE_blendfile_read_from_memory() in WM_init()

```
success = BKE_blendfile_read_from_memory(C,
      datatoc_startup_blend,
      datatoc_startup_blend_size,
      true,
      &(const struct BlendFileReadParams){
          .is_startup = true,
          .skip_flags = skip_flags,
      },
      NULL);
```

Attention should be given to the datatoc_startup_blend formal parameter passed to BKE_blendfile_read_from_memory(). This is the datatoc_startup_blend char array mentioned earlier, defined in *startup.blend.c,* and included by *source/blender/editors/include/ED_datafiles.h* as an externally defined variable.

Note   The module datatoc, located in *source/blender/datatoc/,* produces a separate executable from the blender binary, called *datatoc.* Usage is *datatoc <data_file_from> <data_file_to>.* *datatoc*'s compilation is scripted in the appropriate CMakeLists. txt file and is part of the build process for the Blender system. Once compiled, the build process runs the *datatoc* executable on the blend file from the source repositories' directory under *release/ datafiles/startup.blend.* This produces the *startup.blend.c* file, which is deposited in the build directory outside of the source repository (e.g., in the build directory under its own *release/datafiles/).* It is not just the *startup.blend* file that is converted to c code and baked into the blender executable. You can find the entire list of "data-to-c" variables in *ED_datafiles.h*.

BKE_blendfile_read_from_memory() has a counterpart function called BKE_blendfile_read(), both found in *source/blender/blenkernel/intern/blendfile.c*. The difference is that one is responsible for opening and closing a file in storage and the other directly from memory. However, BKE_blendfile_read_from_memory() is our immediate concern. A pointer to a BlendFileData struct is declared at the top of BKE_blendfile_read_from_memory(). BlendFileData stores the data read from a blend file (either from memory or storage). See Listing 2-8 for details on the BlendFileData struct definition.

Listing 2-8. The BlendFileData struct definition from source/blender/blenloader/BLO_readfile.h

```
typedef struct BlendFileData {
  struct Main *main;
  struct UserDef *user;

  int fileflags;
  int globalf;
  char filename[1024]; /* 1024 = FILE_MAX */

  struct bScreen *curscreen; /* TODO think this isn't needed
  anymore? */
  struct Scene *curscene;
  struct ViewLayer *cur_view_layer; /* layer to activate in
  workspaces when reading without UI */

  eBlenFileType type;
} BlendFileData;
```

43

Clearly, some of the fields from the BlendFileData struct are irrelevant when loading the default blend file from memory (e.g., filename and fileflags). (As of Blender v2.8, the enum eBlenFileType only has a single valid value.) It is actually BLO_read_from_memory() that returns our BlendFileData object, so let us continue there to see what happens.

BLO_read_from_memory() is defined in *source/blender/blenloader/ intern/readblenentry.c.* Here, we further declare a pointer to another struct called FileData. FileData directly deals with the low-level details of file properties. It is still used even when loading from memory, as there is a common function blo_read_file_internal(), defined in *source/blender/ blendloader/intern/readfile.c,* that both execution paths (either loading from memory or from an external file) take. Both BLO_read_from_memory() and BLO_read_from_file() are closely related and mainly handle wrapping calls to the more fundamental function blo_read_file_internal().

Note   Functions that are prefaced with capital letters that abbreviate their respective modules form part of the module's API (i.e., functional interface) for other Blender modules. For example, we have seen this with WM_init(), from the windowmanager API, and BLO_read_ from_file(), etc., from the blenderloader module. Functions that maintain the same abbreviations (e.g., wm_homefile_read() or blo_filedata_from_memory()), but in lowercase, are not meant to be called from outside of the module itself. Their definitions are located in the *intern* directory of the module's top-level directory, whereas the API functions are located just under a module's top-level directory outside of the *intern* subdirectory. "Intern" functions (those internal to the module and defined within *intern*) may be declared with static or extern storage, whereas API functions are always declared extern and their prototypes are declared in header files just above the *intern* subdirectory.

Reading the In-Memory startup.blend File

Currently, our call stack looks like the following: main() -> WM_init() -> wm_homefile_read() -> BKE_blendfile_read_from_memory() -> BLO_read_from_memory(). See Figure 2-2.

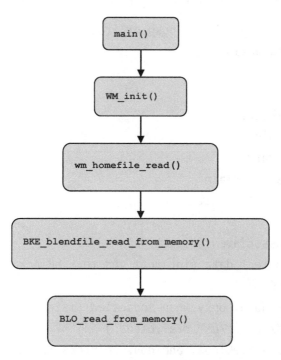

Figure 2-2. Our call sequence from main() to the blendloader module

Notice how calls first go to a module's API and then filter down to internal functions handling more specific conditions and lower-level details of the requests from a module's API.

BLO_read_from_memory() first calls blo_filedata_from_memory(), which returns a FileData struct instance. Here is where we first enter functions defined in *source/blender/blenloader/intern/readfile.c*. At the beginning of *readfile.c*, the approach to reading blend files is documented (see Listing 2-9).

Listing 2-9. Excerpt from a readfile.c comment, describing the algorithm for reading file-blocks (called "LibBlock") from a blend file excluding externally referenced blend files (i.e., "libraries"). As we are interested in the path of execution for the embedded datatoc_ startup_blend char array, this is sufficient for our exploration

```
- Existing Library (#Main) push or free
- allocate new #Main
- load file
- read #SDNA
- for each LibBlock
    - read LibBlock
    - if a Library
        - make a new #Main
        - attach ID's to it
    - else
        - read associated 'direct data'
        - link direct data (internal and to LibBlock)
  - read #FileGlobal
  - read #USER data, only when indicated (file is `~/.config/
  blender/X.XX/config/userpref.blend`)
  - initialize #FileGlobal and copy pointers to #Global
  - free file
  ...
```

The datatoc_startup_blend char array containing the byte contents of the *startup.blend* file is passed to blo_filedata_from_memory(), which reads the first two bytes to determine whether the contents are gzipped. If so, then the reading is aborted. Otherwise, the function pointer fd_read_ from_memory is assigned to a FileData's read field.

You may wonder at what point the data from each blend file-block (libbloc) is first loaded into the FileData object. We need to branch to blo_decode_and_check() from blo_filedata_from_memory(), passing by reference an object of FileData. We visit a few separate functions from blo_decode_and_check(). Firstly, we enter decode_blender_header(), where a hard-coded string, "BLENDER," is checked against the loaded header, along with other chars expected to be present in the file header.

Secondly, we call read_file_dna() from blo_decode_and_check(). This function reads both the global and "DNA" type definitions particular to the version of the blend file, making appropriate byte swaps (big versus little endian) if necessary for these blocks only (later we will do conversions for the other file-blocks, using the *makesdna* API). Along the way, each of the file-blocks is loaded into our FileData object as well, via calls to blo_bhead_next().

After returning from blo_filedata_from_memory(), BLO_read_from_memory() continues to call blo_read_file_internal(), assuming that a non-NULL FileData instance was returned from blo_filedata_from_memory().

It is not until blo_read_file_internal() (see Listing 2-10) that we begin to parse the data-blocks from the blend file format. This function is also in service of any routine that reads blend file information and therefore independent of either storage or memory source. A BlendFileData object will be returned from blo_read_file_internal().

Listing 2-10. blo_read_file_internal()'s case handling for each "DNA" block type. Call to read_libblock() is bolded for significance here

```
...

while (bhead) {
    switch (bhead->code) {
        case DATA:
        case DNA1:
        case TEST: /* used as preview since 2.5x */
```

```
case REND:
  bhead = blo_bhead_next(fd, bhead);
  break;
case GLOB:
  bhead = read_global(bfd, fd, bhead);
  break;
case USER:
  if (fd->skip_flags & BLO_READ_SKIP_USERDEF) {
    bhead = blo_bhead_next(fd, bhead);
  }
  else {
    bhead = read_userdef(bfd, fd, bhead);
  }
  break;
case ENDB:
  bhead = NULL;
  break;

case ID_LINK_PLACEHOLDER:
  if (fd->skip_flags & BLO_READ_SKIP_DATA) {
    bhead = blo_bhead_next(fd, bhead);
  }
  else {
    /* Add link placeholder to the main of the
       library it belongs to.
     * The library is the most recently loaded
       ID_LI block, according
     * to the file format definition. So we can
       use the entry at the
     * end of mainlist, added in
       direct_link_library. */
```

```
    Main *libmain = mainlist.last;
    bhead = read_libblock(fd, libmain, bhead,
                          0, true, NULL);
  }
  break;
/* in 2.50+ files, the file identifier for
   screens is patched, forward compatibility */
case ID_SCRN:
  bhead->code = ID_SCR;
  /* pass on to default */
  ATTR_FALLTHROUGH;
default:
  if (fd->skip_flags & BLO_READ_SKIP_DATA) {
    bhead = blo_bhead_next(fd, bhead);
  }
  else {
    bhead = read_libblock(fd, bfd->main, bhead,
                LIB_TAG_LOCAL, false, NULL);
  }
}
...
```

As shown in Listing 2-9, there are lower-level reader functions called from blo_read_file_internal(). Let us discuss two of them, read_global() and read_libblock(), both static and defined in *readfile.c*. At this level, the static functions no longer have the module prefix (here, the lowercase blo_*). We have seen this already with the function read_file_dna().

read_global() is used to gather version information from the blend file (stored in the GLOB data-block) and is mostly prosaic. It copies this data from our FileData object, into the common BlendFileData object, first created in blo_read_internal() after calling read_struct().

For most file-block codes (excluding the globals, dna, and userdef blocks), we will execute read_libblock(), shown in Listing 2-11.

Listing 2-11. Calls (in bold type) for copying FileData to corresponding "DNA" struct type. and then to the struct Main. This "linking" is also shown in bold type for the Mesh struct

```
static BHead *read_libblock(FileData *fd,
        Main *main,
        BHead *bhead,
        const int tag,
        const bool placeholder_set_indirect_extern,
        ID **r_id)
{
  /* this routine reads a libblock and its direct data. Use
  link functions to connect it all
   */
  ID *id;
...

  /* read libblock */
  id = read_struct(fd, bhead, "lib block");

...

  /* init pointers direct data */
  direct_link_id(fd, id);

...

  switch (GS(id->name)) {
    case ID_WM:
      direct_link_windowmanager(fd,
                          (wmWindowManager *)id);
      break;
```

```
case ID_SCR:
  wrong_id = direct_link_screen(fd,
                        (bScreen*)id);
  break;
case ID_SCE:
  direct_link_scene(fd, (Scene *)id);
  break;
case ID_OB:
  direct_link_object(fd, (Object *)id);
  break;
case ID_ME:
  direct_link_mesh(fd, (Mesh *)id);
  break;
...
```

The ID type simply stores the file-block header information, which is how we distinguish which type of file-block we need to process. read_struct() is then called to fill out the id variable with the file-block header data. It is a static utility function also defined in *readfile.c* and used to direct transformation of the information from a file-block's corresponding DNA serialized struct. It uses version information already stored in a FileData object, which is passed to it. read_struct() checks the SDNA version and converts byte-level variations to the version of Blender reading the file-block, via calls to the *makesdna* module via its DNA_* prefaced API functions—prototyped in *source/blender/makesdna/DNA_genfile.h*.

We skip over descent into the "linking" functions shown in bold type in Listing 2-11. These functions copy pointers from the FileData object storing the converted data version, first into an ID object that represents the file-block header and then an object of the "DNA" struct type represented by its corresponding file-block data (i.e., the fields of the struct) using direct_link_*() where * represents the "DNA" type (mesh case is in bold type in Listing 2-11).

Returning to blo_read_file_internal(), in our BlendFileData local variable called bfd, we copy this DNA struct type into the struct Main via lib_link_all(), shown in Listing 2-12.

Listing 2-12. In blo_read_file_internal(), linking is shown in bold type for the Mesh "DNA" type struct

```
...

if ((fd->skip_flags & BLO_READ_SKIP_DATA) == 0) {
    read_libraries(fd, &mainlist);

    blo_join_main(&mainlist);

    lib_link_all(fd, bfd->main);
...
```

Our BlendFileData object containing a read struct Main is returned from blo_read_file_internal() to BLO_read_from_memory(), which in turn copies it to the calling function BKE_blendfile_read_from_memory(). This, of course, happens after all of the blend file has completed loading. We are still left with copying this struct Main to our struct bContext. This is done through setup_app_blend_file_data(), from BKE_blendfile_read_from_memory(), shown in Listing 2-13.

Listing 2-13. Adding a struct Main to a struct bContext from BKE_blendfile_read_from_memory(), back in blendfile.c

```
bool BKE_blendfile_read_from_memory(bContext *C,
            const void *filebuf,
            int filelength,
            bool update_defaults,
            const struct BlendFileReadParams *params,
            ReportList *reports)
```

```
{
  BlendFileData *bfd;

  bfd = BLO_read_from_memory(filebuf, filelength,
                      params->skip_flags, reports);
  if (bfd) {
    if (update_defaults) {
      if ((params->skip_flags & BLO_READ_SKIP_DATA)
          == 0)
      {
        BLO_update_defaults_startup_blend(bfd->main,
                               NULL);
      }
    }

    setup_app_blend_file_data(C, bfd, "<memory2>",
                               params, reports);
    ...
```

The remaining call sequence is setup_app_blend_file_data(...) -> setup_app_data(...) -> CTX_data_main_set(C, bmain). The setup_* functions are defined in *blendfile.c*.

CTX_* are struct bContext accessor functions defined in *source/blender/blendkernel/intern/context.c. context.c* is located in the *blendkernel* module, and its interface is defined by *BKE_context.h*. However, because of the importance of the struct bContext type, Blender uses the CTX_* prefix instead of the BKE_* prefix on the API to the struct bContext type.

Summary

In this chapter, we introduced aspects of Blender serialization. We also discussed Blender's DNA, and the related modules. There was reference to included documents in the Blender repository, for further description of the blend file format. We showed how to use the Python scripts provided as part of the source repositories' documents.

Lastly, we traced a typical factory startup execution path for loading the embedded blend file. While we did not trace writing to a blend file, this is a worthy exercise. However, an understanding of Blender's operator system is necessary to see how callbacks are set for UI operations. We will look more deeply into operator callbacks and UI in an upcoming chapter.

CHAPTER 3

ghost: Soul of the windowmanager Module

This chapter illustrates the dividing line between "core" Blender source code and one of the most fundamental of Blender's internal support libraries called ghost. We will uncover the connection between ghost and windowmanager, the module that provides the underpinnings for Blender's window-based application. Importantly, Blender is also an OpenGL program. We outline the required steps client programs must undertake to obtain a platform-specific window, along with an associated rendering context. Additionally, we discuss how you may write your own OpenGL application on top of ghost. Following this, we show how the windowmanager itself calls ghost. This allows the windowmanager module to abstract the windowing system, which is part of the underlying operating system.

© Brad E. Hollister 2021
B. E. Hollister, *Core Blender Development*,
https://doi.org/10.1007/978-1-4842-6415-7_3

The Generic Handy Operating System Toolkit (ghost)

A standard practice is to label software artifacts with nifty acronyms, often with somewhat obscure reference to earlier programs. ghost is no exception. The title of this section is the full acronym for ghost: Generic Handy Operating System Toolkit.

Overview

There is evidence in the codebase that Blender started as a GLUT[1] application, before using ghost. Definitive proof is provided in comments from *intern/ghost/GHOST_ISystem.h*. However, what does ghost offer Blender? Its services are also summarized in *GHOST_ISystem.h* (Listing 3-1).

Listing 3-1. ghost's abbreviated introductory description from GHOST_ISystem.h. Services are shown in boldface for emphasis. Incidentally, ghost does not create menu items, as these are constructed using OpenGL and by checking mouse position in Blender's native UI code

```
* In short: everything that Blender needed from GLUT to run on
  all it's supported
* operating systems and some extra's.
* This includes :
*
```

---

[1] GLUT (Graphics Library Utility Toolkit) was an early cross-platform support library for creating operating system-specific windows and an OpenGL rendering context. The original version was written by Mark Kilgard, the author of the "Green Book," i.e., *OpenGL Programming for the X Windows System*. Following Kilgard's GLUT, freeglut was used extensively by the "Red Book" (i.e., the *OpenGL Programming Guide*) until its ninth edition.

```
* - Time(r) management.
* - Display/window management (windows are only created on the
    main display).
* - Event management.
* - Cursor shape management (no custom cursors for now).
* - Access to the state of the mouse buttons and the keyboard.
* - Menus for windows with events generated when they are
    accessed (this is
*   work in progress).
* - Video mode switching.
* - Copy/Paste buffers.
* - System paths.
*
* Font management has been moved to a separate library.
*
```

We will see that ghost directly interfaces with Xlib (X11), Mac OS, or MicroSoft Windows in order to create an application window. Native OS windows are the receivers of events from an operating system. Thus, ghost captures these events, and an application built upon ghost must then implement an appropriate handler routine. We will show examples in an upcoming section.

Both GLUT and GLFW[2] take over an application's event loop, known as "inversion of control." We have already seen in Chapter 1 that Blender's event loop is in the windowmanager module (*source/blender/windowmanager/intern/wm.c*). As a comparison, GLFW is considered a "framework," as the library itself runs the event loop. A client application

---

[2]Today, most introductory texts on OpenGL development use an analog to the GLUT library called GLFW (Graphics Library Framework).

using GLFW must register callback functions with it. In contrast, the `windowmanager` module maintains the event loop for Blender and is written on top of ghost.[3]

Initialization

We will not go into the specifics of creating a window, or obtaining a rendering context for any particular operating system. Nevertheless, the requirements for a client program are as follows:

1. Obtain an application window.

2. Obtain an OpenGL rendering context from the windowing system, for the display (bound by the constraints of the physical display and rendering hardware).

3. Make the rendering context current.

The first step involves getting the display's characteristics and mapping this to the application's window.

Applications may have more than one rendering context. A rendering context represents an instance of the OpenGL state machine. It contains version information, pixel-type data, and the resolution required to instantiate it. All of this is accomplished via an intermediary: GLX, AGL, or WGL. Which one that is used depends on the operating system.

In the third step, applications must tell the operating system when to swap the render buffers. For instance, on X11, this is done with a call to `glXSwapBuffers()`. On Windows platforms, `wglSwapBuffers()` must be used instead. OpenGL, itself, does not perform this.

---

[3]A software "toolkit" does not require such an abstraction of the event loop. However, GLUT also maintained the event loop for applications using it, despite it generally being called a "toolkit."

Like GLUT and GLFW, ghost deals directly with the platform's API. An application using ghost only interacts with ghost, not the platform API. Thus, ghost makes Blender portable and simplifies the duties of the "core" codebase.

Header Files

Figure 3-1 lists the header files for ghost. ghost is written in C++, unlike "core" Blender. Most of its headers declare an abstract class. Exceptions are *GHOST_C-api.h*, *GHOST_Path-api.h*, *GHOST_Rect.h*, and *GHOST_Types.h*.

Figure 3-1. *Top-level* ghost *header files. The majority of these files provide the interface to* ghost*.* ghost *is written in C++. Headers with an "I" preceding the second word in their title, for example, GHOST_ IWindow.h, declare an abstract class*

In the case of *GHOST_C-api.h*, we have a set of function prototypes whose definitions access the underlying class-based objects using an empty struct called a "handle." Two examples are GHOST_SystemHandle and GHOST_WindowHandle. *GHOST_Path-api.h* exports the API for directory information. Directory access is performed by the operating system's programming interface. However, on POSIX (Portable Operating System Interface for Unix), the user (home), binary, and system directories all should be accessed using ghost, with member functions defined in a source file for the appropriate platform.

GHOST_SystemPathsUnix::getUserDir() is a deprecated member function from *GHOST_SystmePathsUnix.cpp (located in intern/ghost/ intern/)*. It works only for Blender versions before 2.64.[4] More recent versions use freedesktop.org.[5] Why would an application need this information? In order to set a starting directory for the Blender file browser, when saving or loading files (e.g., blend files), etc.

GHOST_Rect.h provides the declaration for the GHOST_Rect class. GHOST_Rect implements operations for rectangle objects. Member functions include, but are not limited to, GHOST_Rect::getHeight(), GHOST_Rect::getWidth(), and GHOST_Rect::isValid(). GHOST_Rect is used for mouse coordinate calculations.

GHOST_Types.h implements enums for state, and struct records for holding settings (Listing 3-2). *GHOST_Types.h* also contains enums defining key codes, returned from the operating system.

Listing 3-2. GHOST_TWindowState and GHOST_DisplaySetting, both from GHOST_Types.h

```
typedef enum {
  GHOST_kWindowStateNormal = 0,
  GHOST_kWindowStateMaximized,
  GHOST_kWindowStateMinimized,
  GHOST_kWindowStateFullScreen,
```

---

[4]For versions of Blender prior to 2.64, the POSIX C standard library's interface is imported via <pwd.h> in *GHOST_SystemPathsUnix.cpp*, which provides access to the system file etc/passwd, a text-file database of information about the current user, including the user's home directory.

[5]Formerly X Desktop Group, an open source project providing standard interfaces to desktop environments using X11 windowing systems.

```
GHOST_kWindowStateEmbedded,
// GHOST_kWindowStateModified,
// GHOST_kWindowStateUnModified,
} GHOST_TWindowState;

typedef struct {
    /** Number of pixels on a line. */
    GHOST_TUns32 xPixels;
    /** Number of lines. */
    GHOST_TUns32 yPixels;
    /** Numberof bits per pixel. */
    GHOST_TUns32 bpp;
    /** Refresh rate (in Hertz). */
    GHOST_TUns32 frequency;
} GHOST_DisplaySetting;
```

Dependencies

ghost began as an internal library, whose only dependencies were operating system APIs external to Blender's repository.[6] ghost's internal dependencies are shown in Figure 3-2. Only "drag-and-drop" references *source/blender/imbuf*. The dependency arises from *ghost/intern/GHOST_EventDragDrop.h*, where both *IMB_imbuf.h* and *IMB_imbuf_types.h* are included. ghost's use of *intern/utfconv* is for Windows builds. ghost also depends on *intern/libmv* for motion tracking, when configured for 3D mouse support on Mac OS. This can be disabled with CMake's build variable WITH_INPUT_NDOF.

ghost may leverage the Simple DirectMedia Layer (SDL). However, SDL can also be disabled. This is done via the CMake build variable WITH_SDL.

---

[6]This is noted in the *intern/ghost/GHOST_ISystem.h* comments. See reference to abbreviated comment section in Listing 3-1.

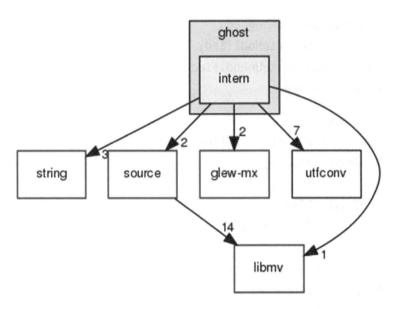

Figure 3-2. *Dependency graph for* ghost *(excluding tests). Arrows point in the direction of dependency. Annotations on directed edges count the count references.[7] Red outlined directories have further dependencies not shown. The dependency on the* imbuf *module is not shown explicitly, but rather as the general dependency on the* [repository root]/source *directory*

Accounting for *intern/utconf, source/blender/imbuf,* and *intern/libmv,* we are left with *intern/string* and *intern/glew-mx.* Figures 3-3 and 3-4 show the directory layout for these dependencies.

GLEW (Graphics Library Extension Wrangler) is an external open source library, used for OpenGL extension functions. The library gathers extensions for an application, as its name suggests. Blender's glew-mx extends GLEW, supporting extensions for multiple rendering contexts. GLEW itself has limited support for this.

Last in the lineup of ghost dependencies, we have string (Figure 3-4). This is a C++ library wrapping much of the C string library (*string.h*).

---

[7]The graph was created using graphviz (graphviz.org) and Doxygen (doxygen.nl).

Figure 3-3. *The intern/glew-mx files. Used by* ghost *to access GLEW and* glew-mx *functionality*

Figure 3-4. *The* string *module files. An object-oriented wrapper for the C string functions*

Classes

Object categories having abstract base classes are

- System

- Window

- Context

- Event

- Timer

These are the elements of ghost's duties. They take care of platform specifics regarding window and rendering context creation for Blender, or even possibly a separate application using ghost. Figure 3-1 shows a listing of the header files in ghost, where interfaces are noted by the inclusion of the letter "I" in the file name. While the interface classes contain pure virtual member function declarations, even GHOST_Rect declares its functions virtual, opening the possibility that this class could be derived from.

As the name implies, GHOST_ISystem is an abstract base class for an object-oriented representation of the operating system. We see its class diagram in Figure 3-5. GHOST_ISystem is instantiated as a singleton. It has a static factory member function called GHOST_ISystem::createSystem(), and a static accessor member function called GHOST_ISystem::getSystem(). Additionally, its constructor is protected, enforcing that only GHOST_ISystem::createSystem() be allowed to create an instance, when called from one of its child class (see Figure 3-5).

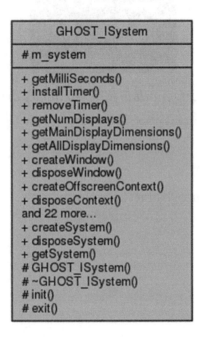

Figure 3-5. *Class diagram for the abstract base class GHOST_ ISystem. The + modifier denotes public members, the # modifier a protected member. This is an interface. It cannot be instantiated. The constructor GHOST_ISystem() is protected. This allows derived classes, using the factory function createSystem(), to instantiate a child class representing an operating system*

GHOST_System inherits from GHOST_ISystem, an abstract class. GHOST_System therefore implements members found in concrete platform classes. Two examples are GHOST_System::getMilliSeconds() and GHOST_System::installTimer(). Figure 3-6 shows diagrams for two of these "system" classes: GHOST_SystemWin32 and GHOST_SystemX11. These represent Windows and X11 systems, respectively.

Figure 3-6. *GHOST_SystemWin32 and GHOST_SystemX11 are two of the concrete "system" classes from intern/ghost/intern/. Their constructor/destructor are public, unlike the parent classes*

The pattern for GHOST_ISystem is similar to the other ghost types Window, Context, Event, and Timer. Note that ghost contains more than just these primary classes.

ghost has its own "window manager" class called GHOST_WindowManager. The main difference between the windowmanager module and GHOST_WindowManager is Blender's module-level concerns. GHOST_WindowManager overlooks windows created at the level of GHOST (the operating system-level windows such as X11 or MacOS). These are returned from the platform API and wrapped by GHOST_WindowWin32, GHOST_WindowX11, GHOST_WindowCocoa, etc. Blender's windowmanager also implements a Blender-specific application window.

The following are "manager" classes, not exposed outside of GHOST, with header files located in *intern/ghost/intern/*:

- GHOST_WindowManager
- GHOST_DisplayManager
- GHOST_EventManager
- GHOST_NDOFManager
- GHOST_TimeManager

Some of these classes are extended for a platform, for example, GHOST_DisplayManager and GHOST_NDOFManager.[8] Another class category is events. GHOST_Button represents a mouse button, used for event state management. GHOST_Button encapsulates such things as "middle mouse-button up." Classes representing events, derived from GHOST_Event, are

- GHOST_EventButton
- GHOST_EventCursor
- GHOST_EventDragDrop
- GHOST_EventKey

---

[8]"NDOF" is used for a 3D Mouse. It can be excluded from a build.

C-API

Blender is written in C. However, ghost is a C++ library. Thus, Blender needs to interface ghost using a function-only interface. This is where *intern/ghost/intern/GHOST_C-api.cpp* and its associated header *intern/ ghost/GHOST_C-api.h* are involved. They work as an adapter for the two-way C to C++ communication. The function prototypes from *GHOST_C-api.h* are akin to the interface encountered with GLUT and GLFW. ghost, however, must be passed an object representing state. There are handles for each of the following types:

- GHOST_System
- GHOST_TimerTask
- GHOST_WindowHandle
- GHOST_EventHandle
- GHOST_RectangleHandle
- GHOST_EventConsumerHandle
- GHOST_ContextHandle

ghost's C API will become more clear, when we cover a sample OpenGL application written in C. We mentioned that the *GHOST_C-api. cpp* functions use "handles," or more specifically, C struct pointers for the ghost object types. These pointers are then cast to their C++ class object counterparts.

The handle declarations are made at the top of the C API header file *intern/ghost/GHOST_C-api.h* (Listing 3-3). Listing 3-4 shows macro template definitions from *intern/ghost/GHOST-Types.h*.

Listing 3-3. In C programs using ghost, handles are C `struct` pointers. In the C++ API implementation, these are cast to C++ object pointers. Parameters passed to the C API functions are transferred to the member functions of the corresponding C++ class. The C `struct` pointer types are in boldface

```
...
GHOST_DECLARE_HANDLE(GHOST_SystemHandle);
GHOST_DECLARE_HANDLE(GHOST_TimerTaskHandle);
GHOST_DECLARE_HANDLE(GHOST_WindowHandle);
GHOST_DECLARE_HANDLE(GHOST_EventHandle);
GHOST_DECLARE_HANDLE(GHOST_RectangleHandle);
GHOST_DECLARE_HANDLE(GHOST_EventConsumerHandle);
GHOST_DECLARE_HANDLE(GHOST_ContextHandle);
...
```

Listing 3-4. GHOST_Types.h's "unguarded" memory version of C `struct` definitions' handles. Macro condition for reference counting is omitted for brevity

```
...
#else
#  define GHOST_DECLARE_HANDLE(name) \
    typedef struct name##__ { \
      int unused; \
    } * name
#endif
```

Representative ghost C API functions using the GHOST_SystemHandle are shown in Listing 3-5. GHOST_SystemHandle is a proxy for child classes derived from GHOST_System (*intern/ghost/intern/GHOST_System.cpp*), for example, GHOST_SystemX11, GHOST_SystemWin32, GHOST_SystemCocoa, etc.

Each is implemented in its own file, located at *intern/ghost/intern/*. The derived ghost system types are named according to the native systems' API: X11, Win32, or Cocoa.

Listing 3-5. A few ghost C API functions using the GHOST_ SystemHandle. GHOST_SystemHandle shown in boldface

```
extern GHOST_SystemHandle GHOST_CreateSystem(void);
extern GHOST_TUns8 GHOST_GetNumDisplays(GHOST_SystemHandle
systemhandle);
extern void GHOST_GetMainDisplayDimensions(GHOST_SystemHandle
systemhandle, GHOST_TUns32 *width, GHOST_TUns32 *height);
extern void GHOST_GetAllDisplayDimensions(GHOST_SystemHandle
systemhandle,GHOST_TUns32 *width, GHOST_TUns32 *height);
extern GHOST_WindowHandle GHOST_CreateWindow(GHOST_SystemHandle
systemhandle, const char *title, GHOST_TInt32 left,
GHOST_TInt32 top, GHOST_TUns32 width, GHOST_TUns32 height,
GHOST_TWindowState state, GHOST_TDrawingContextType type,
GHOST_GLSettings glSettings);
```

An example of the C API function is shown in Listing 3-6. We can see GHOST_SystemHandle cast to its C++ object type. Then, GHOST_ ISystem::createWindow() is passed the C API's parameters. Finally, we encounter GHOST_Window, cast to GHOST_WindowHandle, for the client C program. Notice how GHOST_CreateWindow() takes its parameters and passes them along to GHOST_ISystem::createWindow(). This member function is resolved to the runtime type for the platform, that is, GHOST_ SystemX11, GHOST_SystemWin32, GHOST_SystemCocoa, etc. After this, a call to the appropriate member function from a GHOST_Window-derived class (e.g., GHOST_WindowX11, GHOST_WindowWin32, GHOST_WindowCocoa) is made. Eventually GHOST calls the platform (e.g., API for X11, Win32, Cocoa, etc.).

Listing 3-6. GHOST_CreateWindow() is implemented in intern/ghost/intern/GHOST_C-api.cpp. Here, we see a GHOST_SystemHandle cast to its C++ pointer type GHOST_ISystem. We also see the return type, a pointer to GHOST_IWindow, cast to GHOST_WindowHandle

```
GHOST_WindowHandle GHOST_CreateWindow(GHOST_SystemHandle
systemhandle,
                  const char *title,
                  GHOST_TInt32 left,
                  GHOST_TInt32 top,
                  GHOST_TUns32 width,
                  GHOST_TUns32 height,
                  GHOST_TWindowState state,
                  GHOST_TDrawingContextType type,
                  GHOST_GLSettings glSettings)
{
   GHOST_ISystem *system = (GHOST_ISystem*)
                       systemhandle;

   return (GHOST_WindowHandle)system->createWindow(
         title, left, top, width, height, state,
         type, glSettings, false, false);
}
```

Note   ghost's C API functions work similarly to GHOST_
CreateWindow(). They cast a handle parameter and then make a
polymorphic call on GHOST_ISystem. The correct system class is
responsible for working with an object of the type representing the
current action (such as a Window, Event, etc.). Member function(s)
then call the appropriate platform API. This is the abstraction
mechanism ghost provides client C programs, allowing them to
be written without concern for the underlying operating system.
Listings 3-7 and 3-8 show GHOST_SystemX11's process for creating
a window.

Listing 3-7. GHOST_SystemX11::createWindow() is called by
GHOST_CreateWindow(). Subsequently it calls GHOST_WindowX11's
constructor. This code is implemented by intern/ghost/intern/
GHOST_SystemX11.cpp

```
GHOST_IWindow *GHOST_SystemX11::createWindow(
    const STR_String &title,
    GHOST_TInt32 left,
    GHOST_TInt32 top,
    GHOST_TUns32 width,
    GHOST_TUns32 height,
    GHOST_TWindowState state,
    GHOST_TDrawingContextType type,
    GHOST_GLSettings glSettings,
    const bool exclusive,
    const bool is_dialog,
    const GHOST_IWindow *parentWindow)
```

```
{
  GHOST_WindowX11 *window = NULL;

  if (!m_display)
    return 0;

  window = new GHOST_WindowX11(this,
                    m_display,
                    title,
                    left,
                    top,
                    width,
                    height,
                    state,
                    (GHOST_WindowX11*)
                      parentWindow,
                    type,
                    is_dialog,
                    ((glSettings.flags &
                      GHOST_glStereoVisual) != 0),
                    exclusive,
                    ((glSettings.flags &
                      GHOST_glAlphaBackground) != 0),
                    (glSettings.flags &
                        GHOST_glDebugContext) != 0);

...
```

Listing 3-8. GHOST_WindowX11's constructor. Much of the XVisualInfo and XSetWindowsAttributes setup is not shown. This is where ghost's abstraction ends and calls to X11 are made. The call to XCreateWindow (an X11 API call) is in boldface

```
GHOST_WindowX11::GHOST_WindowX11(GHOST_SystemX11 *system,
      Display *display,
      const STR_String &title,
      GHOST_TInt32 left,
      GHOST_TInt32 top,
      GHOST_TUns32 width,
      GHOST_TUns32 height,
      GHOST_TWindowState state,
      GHOST_WindowX11 *parentWindow,
      GHOST_TDrawingContextType type,
      const bool is_dialog,
      const bool stereoVisual,
      const bool exclusive,
      const bool alphaBackground,
      const bool is_debug) : GHOST_Window(width, height, state,
      stereoVisual, exclusive),
      m_display(display),
      m_visualInfo(NULL),
      m_fbconfig(NULL),
      m_normal_state(GHOST_kWindowStateNormal),
      m_system(system),
      m_invalid_window(false),
      m_empty_cursor(None),
      m_custom_cursor(None),
      m_visible_cursor(None),
      m_taskbar("blender.desktop"),

...
```

```
/* create the window! */
  if ((parentWindow == 0) || is_dialog) {
    m_window = XCreateWindow(m_display,
                             RootWindow(m_display,
                             m_visualInfo->screen),
                             left,
                             top,
                             width,
                             height,
                             0, /* no border. */
                             m_visualInfo->depth,
                             InputOutput,
                             m_visualInfo->visual,
                             xattributes_valuemask,
                             &xattributes);
```

Minimal OpenGL Program Written in C Using ghost

In order to best understand the ghost C API, let us look at a sample OpenGL program's event loop, and ghost initialization. The full sample program and required CMake files are included with the source code for this book. This provides a foundation for understanding the windowmanager module.

Listing 3-9 shows main(). There, we see the event loop and how events are processed using ghost. The registered callback processEvent() is called by ghost. Notice the client program does not contain code specific to an operating system API. Nor does it directly create an OpenGL rendering context, as that is all accomplished by a call to GHOST_ CreateWindow().

Listing 3-9. A minimal OpenGL application's `main()` function, modified from intern/ghost/test/gears/GHOST_C-Test.c.[9] Each call to ghost is in boldface. We focus on the instantiation of the "event consumer," or callback, that is invoked when `GHOST_DispatchEvent()` is called to "pump" the operating system for the events assigned to the application window created via `GHOST_CreateWindow()`. The `main()` function is abbreviated, excluding shader registration, OpenGL initialization, timer callback registration, and disposing of the system object by the appropriate calls to ghost

```
int main(int argc, char **argv)
{
  GHOST_GLSettings glSettings = {0};
  char *title1 = "Main Window";
  GHOST_EventConsumerHandle consumer =
    GHOST_CreateEventConsumer(processEvent, NULL);

  /* Create the system */
  shSystem = GHOST_CreateSystem();
  GHOST_AddEventConsumer(shSystem, consumer);

  if (shSystem) {
    /* Create the main window */
```

[9]It should be noted that the *GHOST_C-Test.c* uses immediate mode OpenGL calls and a fixed function pipeline. Thus, with OpenGL versions above 3.0, *GHOST_C-Test.c* will not work.

```
    sMainWindow = GHOST_CreateWindow(shSystem,
                                     title1,
                                     10,
                                     64,
                                     320,
                                     200,
                         GHOST_kWindowStateNormal,
                GHOST_kDrawingContextTypeOpenGL,
                                     glSettings);

    if (!sMainWindow) {
      printf("could not create main window\n");
      exit(-1);
    }

    ...

    /* Enter main loop */
    while (!sExitRequested) {
      if (!GHOST_ProcessEvents(shSystem, 0)) {
#ifdef WIN32
        /* If there were no events, be nice to other
        applications */
        Sleep(10);
#endif
      }
      GHOST_DispatchEvents(shSystem);
    }
  }

  ...

  return 0;
}
```

windowManager Revisit

Let us continue our journey of Blender's "core" codebase. We look at windowmanager, its use as an abstraction layer, and its interface provided by *WM_api.h*. We will trace the initialization of the application window and the entry into the event loop. ghost is responsible for events, but only at a low level relative to windowmanager.

We saw an example of operators in Chapter 1, a Blender construct to manage event handling. The windowmanager provides a central hub to integrate higher abstraction by the Blender program.

windowManager's ghost-Related Files

Figure 3-7 shows files just under the windowmanager directory (*source/ blender/windowmanager*). We focus our attention on the WM_* API and also how windowmanager maps ghost's functionality to other parts of Blender.

Figure 3-7. *windowmanager's top-level headers and subfolders located in [repository root]/source/blender/windowmanager*

Note   Figure 3-7 shows that windowmanager's header layout is very similar to the other modules, including ghost. It has a "types" header and an "API" header. All functions external to a module are prefaced by capitals, for example, ghost and the windowmanager have GHOST_* and WM_* prefixes for their API, respectively.

---

windowmanager files containing headers from ghost:

- *wm_init_exit.c*

- *wm_window.c*

- *wm_draw.c*

- *wm_event_system.c*

- *wm_files.c (contains GHOST_Path-api.h)*

- *wm_platform_support.c*

- *wm_playanim.c*

- *wm_stereo.c*

- *wm_window_private.h (includes GHOST_Types.h only)*

Each of these files includes *GHOST_C-api.h*, which we inspected earlier. As *GHOST_C-api.h* includes *GHOST_Types.h,* separate inclusion is unnecessary. *GHOST_C-api.h* provides access to the ghost API.

ghost Initialization and Event Registration

In Listing 3-10, we see the initialization of ghost via WM_init(),[10] defined in *wm_init_exit.c.* A bContext parameter holds the state of the entire Blender application—much as a rendering context stores OpenGL state. It is passed to wm_ghost_init(). There, this variable is passed to GHOST_ CreateEventConsumer(). See Listing 3-11.

Listing 3-10. WM_init() calls wm_ghost_init() to initialize ghost. It passes a pointer to the bContext struct discussed in Chapter 2. There is a direct call to the ghost API, which uses GHOST_ CreateSystemPaths()

```
/* only called once, for startup */
void WM_init(bContext *C, int argc, const char **argv)
{

  if (!G.background) {
    wm_ghost_init(C); /* note: it assigns C to ghost! */
```

---

[10]We went over the execution path reaching WM_init() from Blender's main entry point (*source/creator/creator.c*) in Chapter 2, regarding the "startup" blend file.

```
  wm_init_cursor_data();
  BKE_sound_jack_sync_callback_set(sound_jack_sync_callback);
}

GHOST_CreateSystemPaths();

...
```

Listing 3-11. The wm_ghost_init() function from windowmanager/intern/wm_window.c

```
void wm_ghost_init(bContext *C)
{
  if (!g_system) {
    GHOST_EventConsumerHandle consumer;

    if (C != NULL) {
      consumer = GHOST_CreateEventConsumer
                   (ghost_event_proc, C);
    }

    g_system = GHOST_CreateSystem();
    GHOST_SystemInitDebug(g_system, G.debug & G_DEBUG_GHOST);

    if (C != NULL) {
      GHOST_AddEventConsumer(g_system, consumer);
    }

    if (wm_init_state.native_pixels) {
      GHOST_UseNativePixels();
    }

    GHOST_UseWindowFocus(wm_init_state.window_focus);

    WM_init_tablet_api();
  }
}
```

GHOST_CreateEventConsumer() registers an application callback ghost_event_proc. The global variable g_system, a GHOST_SystemHandle instance pointing back to the appropriate class type instance, for the operating system is used in wm_window_process_events(). This occurs in *wm_window.c* during the event loop from *wm.c*—see Chapter 1 (Listing 1-7). We can see wm_window_process_events() in Listing 3-12. This sequence of C API calls is analogous to the minimal C program shown in Listing 3-9, but spread over multiple source files and functions in the windowmanager module.

Listing 3-12. The wm_window_process_events() function found in windowmanager/intern/wm_window.c. This function encapsulates Blender's event "pump"

```
void wm_window_process_events(const bContext *C)
{
  int hasevent;

  BLI_assert(BLI_thread_is_main());

  hasevent = GHOST_ProcessEvents(g_system, 0); /* 0 is no wait */

  if (hasevent) {
    GHOST_DispatchEvents(g_system);
  }
  hasevent |= wm_window_timer(C);

  /* no event, we sleep 5 milliseconds */
  if (hasevent == 0) {
    PIL_sleep_ms(5);
  }
}
```

There is an upcoming discussion, in a later chapter, on how windows are managed by the use of the `wmWindowManager` struct. The `wmWindowManager` struct is defined in *DNA_windowmanager_types.h*, from the `makesdna` module.

Summary

This chapter covered `ghost`. How it abstracts the operating system and OpenGL rendering contexts were essential topics. We first reviewed the steps necessary to write an OpenGL program and how those steps are operating system dependent. GLUT and GLFW are lightweight platform-abstracting "toolkits" that help to offload such steps from a client program. GLEW obtains extension functions for an OpenGL hardware implementation. GLEW, together with GLFW or GLUT, is often used by small OpenGL applications.

Blender does not leverage GLUT—as it once did—but uses `ghost` and `ghost`'s helper libraries, `glew-mx` and `string`. Both of these are maintained internally by Blender's repository. In addition to `ghost`'s file structure and classes, we looked at its C API. Blender is a C program, and `ghost` is written in C++. Therefore, `ghost` has a C API to allow Blender to interface with it.

CHAPTER 4

The **blenlib** and **blenkernel** Modules

In this chapter, we discuss Blender's two largest "core" utility libraries.
blenlib and blenkernel are the primary modules for generic processing
and data. As such, they share a history in the Blender codebase. When
appropriate, we will use Blender's unit tests—written with Google Test[1]—
to survey blenlib's interface (BLI_* functions). Recall struct bContext
is defined in blenkernel. We looked at the CTX_* API, a subset of the
blenkernel API in Chapter 2. blenkernel's API is generally accessed
by BKE_* functions, which comprise a larger portion of its interface.
blenkernel offloads data handling for makesdna, by operating on "DNA"
data types. Other utility modules, namely, blenloader, blenfont, and
blentranslation, are more specialized and beyond the scope of the
current chapter.

---

[1]An xUnit framework written by Google for C++ (and C) programs.

© Brad E. Hollister 2021
B. E. Hollister, *Core Blender Development*,
https://doi.org/10.1007/978-1-4842-6415-7_4

Overview of `blenlib`

The `blenlib` module is quoted by the official documentation as:

> *Internal misc libraries: math functions, lists, random, noise, memory pools, file operations (platform agnostic)*

—https://wiki.blender.org/wiki/
Source/File_Structure

blenlib's dependencies are shown in Figure 4-1. Many other modules are themselves dependent on `blenlib` (Figure 4-2).

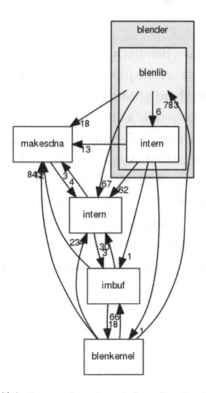

Figure 4-1. `blenlib`'s *dependencies. It has limited dependency on other modules. There is some reliance on the repository's internal support libraries, shown in the red*

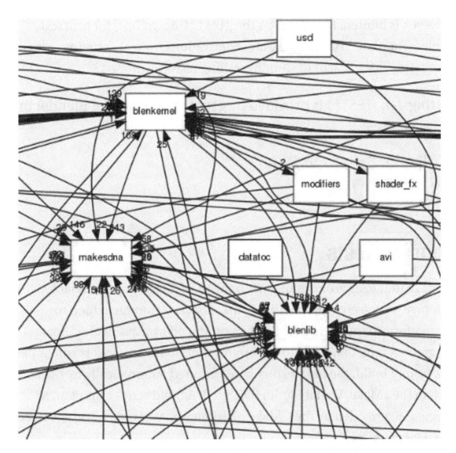

Figure 4-2. *Partial dependency graph for both* blenlib *and* blenkernel*. Note that* blenlib*,* blenlib*, and* makesdna *each have a relatively high number of dependent modules*

Google Test

One approach to exploring blenlib is to read the unit tests from *source/blender/blenlib/tests/*. Almost every source file in *source/blender/blenlib/intern/* has a corresponding test file having .cc extension.

First, we will need to briefly describe Google Test and to a lesser extent CMake's CTest facility. The Blender source tree contains unit tests for functions at the module API level. The number of modules tested, however, is limited. Blender uses the gtest (Google Test) for unit test implementation. Test cases are class derivations from gtest's Test class. gtest provides a macro to simplify writing tests (Listing 4-1).

Listing 4-1. TEST() is provided by gtest. The format of Blender unit tests is shown

```
TEST(TestSuiteName, TestName) {
    ... test body ...
}
```

Running Tests

blenlib unit tests are compiled with the WITH_GTESTS option enabled in *source/blender/blenlibblenlib/CMakeLists.txt*. They are added to the platform-dependent build scripts produced by running the CMake program. A target is added to the build script, so that when it is run as part of a system build, the unit tests can be executed automatically by the build system (i.e., Make, Visual Studio IDE, etc.). A build script calls *ctest*, an executable provided by the CMake distribution. *ctest* runs tests registered by *CMakeLists.txt*.

Listing 4-2. Partial listing for source/blender/blenlibblenlib/ CMakeLists.txt. Note that the tests are compiled into a single executable blenlib_tests. This executable is written to the build directory in bin/tests/

```
...
if(WITH_GTESTS)
  set(TEST_SRC
    tests/BLI_array_store_test.cc
    tests/BLI_array_test.cc
    tests/BLI_array_utils_test.cc
```

```
tests/BLI_delaunay_2d_test.cc
```
...

It is not necessary to use *ctest*, in order to run unit tests. Unit tests are compiled to the build directory, in *bin/tests/*. All tests are compiled into *blenlib_tests*.

blenlib's Unit Tests

In addition to gtests macros for assertions, Blender adds some for data types defined in blendlib (Listing 4-3). An example is EXPECT_V3_NEAR(), used for three-dimensional vector data types, defined in terms of EXPECT_NEAR()—a gtest macro.

Listing 4-3. Excerpt from tests/gtests/testing/testing.h. EXPECT_NEAR() is used for testing vector data

```
#ifndef __BLENDER_TESTING_H__
#define __BLENDER_TESTING_H__

#include <vector>

#include "gflags/gflags.h"
#include "glog/logging.h"
#include "gtest/gtest.h"

namespace blender::tests {

/* These strings are passed on the CLI with the --test-asset-
dir and --test-release-dir arguments.
 * The arguments are added automatically when invoking tests
via `ctest`. */
const std::string &flags_test_asset_dir();   /* ../lib/tests in
the SVN directory. */
```

```
const std::string &flags_test_release_dir(); /* bin/{blender
version} in the build directory. */

}  // namespace blender::tests

#define EXPECT_V3_NEAR(a, b, eps) \
  { \
    EXPECT_NEAR(a[0], b[0], eps); \
    EXPECT_NEAR(a[1], b[1], eps); \
    EXPECT_NEAR(a[2], b[2], eps); \
  } \
  (void)0

#define EXPECT_V4_NEAR(a, b, eps) \
  { \
    EXPECT_NEAR(a[0], b[0], eps); \
    EXPECT_NEAR(a[1], b[1], eps); \
    EXPECT_NEAR(a[2], b[2], eps); \
    EXPECT_NEAR(a[3], b[3], eps); \
  } \
  (void)0
```

...

As an example of a unit test from *BLI_array_test.cc* (Listing 4-4), we see a test of Array, using the TEST() macro.

Listing 4-4. Partial unit test defined in source/blender/blenlib/ tests/tests/BLI_array_test.cc. blenlib's Array template class is tested

```
#include "BLI_array.hh"
#include "BLI_exception_safety_test_utils.hh"
#include "BLI_strict_flags.h"
#include "BLI_vector.hh"
```

```
#include "testing/testing.h"

namespace blender::tests {

TEST(array, DefaultConstructor)
{
  Array<int> array;
  EXPECT_EQ(array.size(), 0);
  EXPECT_TRUE(array.is_empty());
}

TEST(array, SizeConstructor)
{
  Array<int> array(5);
  EXPECT_EQ(array.size(), 5);
  EXPECT_FALSE(array.is_empty());
}
...
```

blenlib's API

The unit test files for `blenlib` are shown in Figure 4-3. We see that each unit test file roughly corresponds to `blenlib`'s API headers. The file listing in Figure 4-4 is considerably larger, suggesting that the `blenlib` API is not fully tested. Notable omissions: *BLI_convexhull_2D.h, BLI_allocator.h,* and *BLI_timer.h.*

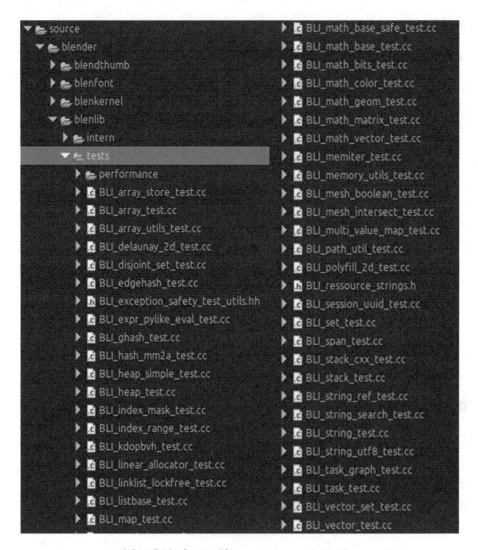

Figure 4-3. *The* blenlib (BLI_*) *unit tests. Each file roughly corresponds to the interface files shown in Figure 4-4*

Figure 4-4. blenlib's interface headers. These files prototype BLI_* functions

Note   While it is virtually impossible to list the entire BLI_* API here, a good way to access documentation separate from the source code is by using Doxygen-generated hyperlinked documents. Doxygen produces pdf or html from JavaDoc-style comments. However, most of the blenlib module's API is not commented, and in many instances its API is either inlined (with a definition in the header only) or simply a preprocessor macro. Most source files in *source/blender/blenlib/intern/* contain statically linked function definitions (e.g., bli_* functions or lower-level helper functions). These are called only indirectly by blenlib's API. The repository provides a Doxygen configuration (*doc/doxygen/Doxyfile*), ready to run on the source. The configuration may be used at the command prompt via doxygen Doxyfile. Doxygen must first be installed.

Features of the **blenlib** API

Parts of blenlib are implemented in C++.[2] Areas of blenlib's concerns are

- Data structures

  - Linked lists

  - Maps

  - Sets

  - kdtree

  - Bounding-volume hierarchy (bvh)

---

[2]Thus, blenlib has utility "mixin" classes, i.e., classes not viable on their own. "Mixins" use multiple inheritance to combine member data and functions between more than one class type.

- Graph algorithms

  - A* search

- Memory allocation

- Hashing

  - Open addressing

  - md5

  - mm2

  - mm3

- Dynamic strings

- Assertions

- Byte swapping for big- and little-endian conversions

- Command-line argument processing

- File operations, such as renaming files

- Path processing for files

- Sorting

- Thread management

- Timers

- Two-dimensional processing

  - Geometry, that is, "rectangles"

  - Noise generation (texture generation)

  - Polygon fill

  - Voronoi

  - UV projection

- Operating system–specific data types

- Bitmaps

- Console output

- Random number generation

- Vector and quaternion math utility functions

    - Higher-order uses of basic functions for "easing" (animation)

    - Convex hull (geometry) processing

    - Color

    - Matrix operations

    - Statistics

    - Rotation

    - Interpolation

    - Quadrics

- Voxels

blenlib implements byte operations (e.g., big- and little-endian conversion, etc.) used for blend files (see Chapter 2). As a reminder, blend files are essentially binary serializations of Blender "DNA."

There are a few surprises. For instance, one is blenlib's dynamic string type struct DynStr, defined in *BLI_dynstr.c*. (We have already seen that there is an internal library called string.) Another is that *BLI_listbase.h* has a dependency on *DNA_listbase.h*, where the functions used to insert and remove from Listbase are prototyped.

Note   `blenlib` contains some redundancy. For linked-lists there are *BLI_linklist.h* and its associated *BLI_link_utils.h*, vs. *BLI_listbase.h* and *BLI_listbase_wrapper.h*. Both provide very similar utilities for `Listbase`. These are essentially two separate linked-list implementations.

`blenlib` API Examples

Now for some API examples. We use Doxygen-derived call graphs to see where calls are made to the API. We also look at API function definitions.

equals_m4m4(), our first example, has its prototype in *source/blender/blenlib/BLI_math_matrix.h* and definition in *source/blender/blenlib/intern/math_matrix.c*. There are no comments in the codebase for equals_ m4m4(). equals_m4m4()'s implementation is shown in Listing 4-5.

Listing 4-5. equals_m4m4() takes two-dimensional arrays of const floats. The function compares each column using equals_v4v4(). If all corresponding column vectors of two 4x4 matrices have identical entries, then matrices are considered equal. A boolean value is returned

```
bool equals_m4m4(const float mat1[4][4], const float mat2[4][4])
{
        return (equals_v4v4(mat1[0], mat2[0]) &&
        equals_v4v4(mat1[1], mat2[1]) &&
        equals_v4v4(mat1[2], mat2[2]) && equals_v4v4(mat1[3],
        mat2[3]));
}
```

equals_m4m4() calls the vector utility function equals_v4v4(), as shown in Listing 4-6. We can see that equals_m4m4() calls equals_v4v4(). Only three functions from the codebase reference equals_m4m4(), shown in Figure 4-5. We see later that the Python interface provides access to equals_m4m4(). Therefore, it is used more frequently than suggested.

Listing 4-6. The equals_v4v4() function. equals_v4v4() is inlined. This is specified by MINLINE, defined as static inline

```
MINLINE bool equals_v4v4(const float v1[4], const float v2[4])
{
    return ((v1[0] == v2[0]) && (v1[1] == v2[1]) && (v1[2] ==
    v2[2]) && (v1[3] == v2[3]));
}
```

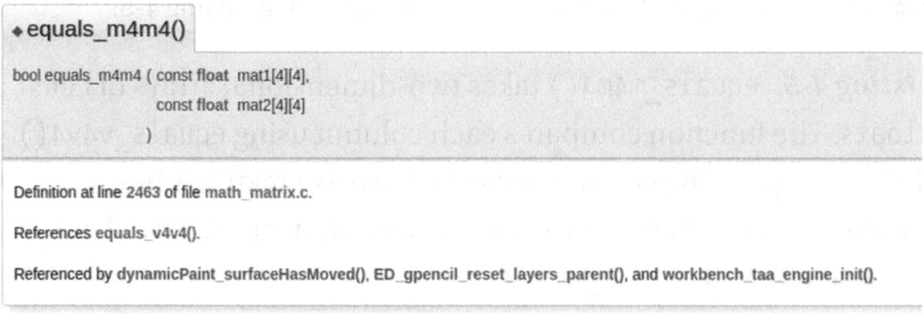

◆ equals_m4m4()

```
bool equals_m4m4 ( const float mat1[4][4],
                   const float mat2[4][4]
                 )
```

Definition at line 2463 of file math_matrix.c.

References equals_v4v4().

Referenced by dynamicPaint_surfaceHasMoved(), ED_gpencil_reset_layers_parent(), and workbench_taa_engine_init().

Figure 4-5. *Doxygen documentation for equals_m4m4()*

Next we have the *BLI_stack.h* API. First, look at struct BLI_Stack, defined in *source/blender/blenlib/intern/stack.c*. BLI_Stack is shown in Figure 4-6 and Listing 4-7.

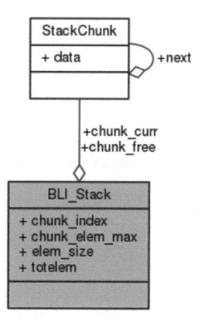

Figure 4-6. *BLI_Stack is an aggregate of StackChunk objects. The open diamond denotes this as an aggregation, not composition. We may have a BLI_Stack object without the need for any StackChunk objects composing the BLI_Stack, that is, the stack can be empty*

Listing 4-7. The BLI_Stack and StackChunk structs from source/ blender/blenlib/intern/stack.c. CHUNK_EMPTY, CHUNK_SIZE_DEFAULT, and CHUNK_ELEM_MIN definitions are shown. In the CHUNK_EMPTY macro, the negative one is cast to size_t (unsigned int). The size_t data type is returned from the sizeof()

```
#define USE_TOTELEM

#define CHUNK_EMPTY ((size_t)-1)
/* target chunks size: 64kb */
#define CHUNK_SIZE_DEFAULT (1 << 16)
/* ensure we get at least this many elems per chunk */
#define CHUNK_ELEM_MIN 32
```

```
struct StackChunk {
  struct StackChunk *next;
  char data[0];
};

struct BLI_Stack {
  struct StackChunk *chunk_curr; /* currently active chunk */
  struct StackChunk *chunk_free; /* free chunks */
  size_t chunk_index;            /* index into 'chunk_curr' */
  size_t chunk_elem_max;         /* number of elements per chunk */
  size_t elem_size;
#ifdef USE_TOTELEM
  size_t totelem;
#endif
};
```

The interface for BLI_Stack operations is found in *BLI_stack.h* (Listing 4-8).

Listing 4-8. Elided BLI_stack.h. Operation names are in boldface. ATTR_WARN_UNUSED_RESULT and ATTR_NONNULL() are defined in source/blender/blenlib/BLI_compiler_attrs.h. They specify attributes that can be verified at compile-time. For instance, with ATTR_NONNULL(), all arguments are checked by the compiler to be non-null. In the absence of any arguments to the macro, only pointers are checked to be non-null

```
...
typedef struct BLI_Stack BLI_Stack;

BLI_Stack *BLI_stack_new_ex(const size_t elem_size,
                            const char *description,
                            const size_t chunk_size) ATTR_WARN_
                            UNUSED_RESULT ATTR_NONNULL();
```

```
BLI_Stack *BLI_stack_new(const size_t elem_size, const char
*description) ATTR_WARN_UNUSED_RESULT
    ATTR_NONNULL();

void BLI_stack_free(BLI_Stack *stack) ATTR_NONNULL();

void *BLI_stack_push_r(BLI_Stack *stack) ATTR_WARN_UNUSED_
RESULT ATTR_NONNULL();
void BLI_stack_push(BLI_Stack *stack, const void *src) ATTR_
NONNULL();

void BLI_stack_pop_n(BLI_Stack *stack, void *dst, unsigned int
n) ATTR_NONNULL();
void BLI_stack_pop_n_reverse(BLI_Stack *stack, void *dst,
unsigned int n) ATTR_NONNULL();
void BLI_stack_pop(BLI_Stack *stack, void *dst) ATTR_NONNULL();

void *BLI_stack_peek(BLI_Stack *stack) ATTR_WARN_UNUSED_RESULT
ATTR_NONNULL();
void BLI_stack_discard(BLI_Stack *stack) ATTR_NONNULL();
void BLI_stack_clear(BLI_Stack *stack) ATTR_NONNULL();

size_t BLI_stack_count(const BLI_Stack *stack) ATTR_WARN_
UNUSED_RESULT ATTR_NONNULL();

bool BLI_stack_is_empty(const BLI_Stack *stack) ATTR_WARN_
UNUSED_RESULT ATTR_NONNULL();
...
```

BLI_stack_pop(), shown in Listing 4-9, has a number of references in the codebase (Figure 4-7). A bmesh operator function calls it from bm_face_split(), defined in *source/blender/bmesh/operators/bmo_dissolve.c*. The BLI_* API is used extensively throughout the codebase.

Listing 4-9. BLI_stack_pop(), from source/blender/blenlib/ intern/stack.c. The code uses BLI_assert() and stack_get_last_ element() for retrieving the top element; that is, a "chunk" of bytes, of elem_size and type struct StackChunk

...

```
static void *stack_get_last_elem(BLI_Stack *stack)
{
  return ((char *)(stack)->chunk_curr->data) + ((stack)->elem_
  size * (stack)->chunk_index);
}
```

...

```
/**
 * Retrieves and removes the top element from the stack.
 * The value is copies to \a dst, which must be at least \a
elem_size bytes.
 *
 * Does not reduce amount of allocated memory.
 */
void BLI_stack_pop(BLI_Stack *stack, void *dst)
{
  BLI_assert(BLI_stack_is_empty(stack) == false);

  memcpy(dst, stack_get_last_elem(stack), stack->elem_size);

  BLI_stack_discard(stack);
}
```

...

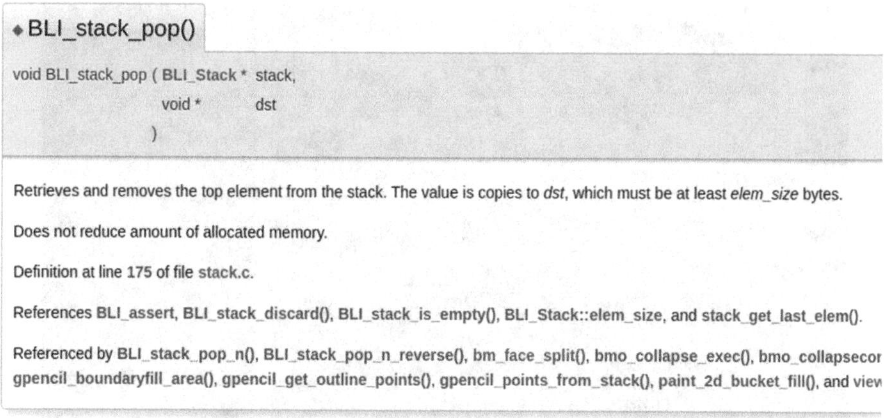

```
♦ BLI_stack_pop()

void BLI_stack_pop ( BLI_Stack *  stack,
                     void *       dst
                   )
```

Retrieves and removes the top element from the stack. The value is copies to *dst*, which must be at least *elem_size* bytes.

Does not reduce amount of allocated memory.

Definition at line 175 of file stack.c.

References BLI_assert, BLI_stack_discard(), BLI_stack_is_empty(), BLI_Stack::elem_size, and stack_get_last_elem().

Referenced by BLI_stack_pop_n(), BLI_stack_pop_n_reverse(), bm_face_split(), bmo_collapse_exec(), bmo_collapsecor gpencil_boundaryfill_area(), gpencil_get_outline_points(), gpencil_points_from_stack(), paint_2d_bucket_fill(), and viev

Figure 4-7. *Documentation for* BLI_stack_pop(). BLI_stack_pop() *is referenced by other BLI_* functions and from the broader codebase*

Overview of **blenkernel**

Unfortunately, blenkernel currently does not have unit tests. We must review its directory and inspect its code directly. From official Blender documentation, the blenkernel module's purpose is:

> *Kernel functions (data structure manipulation, allocation, free. No tools or UI stuff, very low level); kernel functions are shared with the blenderplayer, for loading data*

—https://wiki.blender.org/wiki/
Source/File_Structure

Consider the byte-swapping functions prototyped in *BLI_endian_switch.h*. It might be argued that these functions are low-level enough to reside in blenkernel. (blenkernel's API headers are shown in Figure 4-8.) However, blenkernel's data management routines are specific to Blender. For example, struct bContext (as indicated by *BKE_context.h*) is a Blender construct. Because blenkernel is tightly coupled with other parts of the Blender application codebase, it is difficult to describe the "kernel" functions without also dissecting the modules they assist.

101

blenkernel
▶ intern
▶ BKE_action.h
▶ BKE_addon.h
▶ BKE_anim.h
▶ BKE_animsys.h
▶ BKE_appdir.h
▶ BKE_armature.h
▶ BKE_autoexec.h
▶ BKE_blender_copybuffer.h
▶ BKE_blender_undo.h
▶ BKE_blender_user_menu.h
▶ BKE_blender_version.h
▶ BKE_blender.h
▶ BKE_blendfile.h
▶ BKE_boids.h
▶ BKE_bpath.h
▶ BKE_brush.h
▶ BKE_bvhutils.h
▶ BKE_cachefile.h
▶ BKE_callbacks.h
▶ BKE_camera.h
▶ BKE_ccg.h
▶ BKE_cdderivedmesh.h
▶ BKE_cloth.h
▶ BKE_collection.h
▶ BKE_collision.h
▶ BKE_colorband.h
▶ BKE_colortools.h
▶ BKE_constraint.h
▶ BKE_context.h
▶ BKE_crazyspace.h
▶ BKE_curve.h
▶ BKE_curveprofile.h
▶ BKE_customdata_file.h
▶ BKE_customdata.h
▶ BKE_data_transfer.h
▶ BKE_deform.h
▶ BKE_DerivedMesh.h
▶ BKE_displist_tangent.h
▶ BKE_displist.h
▶ BKE_dynamicpaint.h

▶ BKE_editmesh_cache.h
▶ BKE_editmesh_tangent.h
▶ BKE_editmesh.h
▶ BKE_effect.h
▶ BKE_fcurve.h
▶ BKE_fluid.h
▶ BKE_font.h
▶ BKE_freestyle.h
▶ BKE_global.h
▶ BKE_gpencil_modifier.h
▶ BKE_gpencil.h
▶ BKE_icons.h
▶ BKE_idcode.h
▶ BKE_idprop.h
▶ BKE_image_save.h
▶ BKE_image.h
▶ BKE_ipo.h
▶ BKE_kelvinlet.h
▶ BKE_key.h
▶ BKE_keyconfig.h
▶ BKE_lattice.h
▶ BKE_layer.h
▶ BKE_lib_id.h
▶ BKE_lib_override.h
▶ BKE_lib_query.h
▶ BKE_lib_remap.h
▶ BKE_library.h
▶ BKE_light.h
▶ BKE_lightprobe.h
▶ BKE_linestyle.h
▶ BKE_main_idmap.h
▶ BKE_main.h
▶ BKE_mask.h
▶ BKE_material.h
▶ BKE_mball_tessellate.h
▶ BKE_mball.h
▶ BKE_mesh_iterators.h
▶ BKE_mesh_mapping.h
▶ BKE_mesh_mirror.h
▶ BKE_mesh_remap.h
▶ BKE_mesh_remesh_voxel.h

▶ BKE_mesh_tangent.h
▶ BKE_mesh.h
▶ BKE_modifier.h
▶ BKE_movieclip.h
▶ BKE_multires.h
▶ BKE_nla.h
▶ BKE_node.h
▶ BKE_object_deform.h
▶ BKE_object_facemap.h
▶ BKE_object.h
▶ BKE_ocean.h
▶ BKE_outliner_treehash.h
▶ BKE_packedFile.h
▶ BKE_paint.h
▶ BKE_particle.h
▶ BKE_pbvh.h
▶ BKE_pointcache.h
▶ BKE_report.h
▶ BKE_rigidbody.h
▶ BKE_scene.h
▶ BKE_screen.h
▶ BKE_sequencer.h
▶ BKE_shader_fx.h
▶ BKE_shrinkwrap.h
▶ BKE_softbody.h
▶ BKE_sound.h
▶ BKE_speaker.h
▶ BKE_studiolight.h
▶ BKE_subdiv_ccg.h
▶ BKE_subdiv_deform.h
▶ BKE_subdiv_eval.h
▶ BKE_subdiv_foreach.h
▶ BKE_subdiv_mesh.h
▶ BKE_subdiv_topology.h
▶ BKE_subdiv.h
▶ BKE_subsurf.h
▶ BKE_text_suggestions.h
▶ BKE_text.h
▶ BKE_texture.h
▶ BKE_tracking.h

Figure 4-8. *Partial listing of the* `blenkernel` *module's interface header files. These files prototype the* BKE_* *functions*

Parts of the blenkernel module, such as those dealing with fluids (*BKE_fluid.h, inter/fluid.c*), character animation (*BKE_anim.h, BKE_animsys.h, BKE_armature.h, intern/anim.c, intern/animsys.c, intern/armature.c*), and other specialized areas, are peripheral to our exploration.

DNA Types and **blenkernel**

Most of makesdna's data types have corresponding blenkernel API functions and associated files. These are listed in Table 4-1. blenkernel offers utilities for manipulating makesdna data types. Blender "DNA," which is passed from one module to another, is operated on by functions from blenkernel.

Table 4-1. makesdna *files and their* blenkernel *associated headers. Each BKE_*.h file contains API prototypes. These functions operate on corresponding data types defined in DNA_*.h.*

makesdna File	**blenkernel** File
DNA_action_types.h	*BKE_action.h*
DNA_anim_types.h	*BKE_anim.h*
DNA_boid_types.h	*BKE_boids.h*
DNA_brush_types.h	*BKE_brush.h*
DNA_cachefile_types.h	*BKE_cachefile.h*
DNA_camera_types.h	*BKE_camera.h*
DNA_cloth_types.h	*BKE_cloth.h*
DNA_collection_types.h	*BKE_collection.h*
DNA_color_types.h	*BKE_colortools.h*

(*continued*)

Table 4-1. (*continued*)

makesdna File	blenkernel File
DNA_constraint_types.h	BKE_constraint.h
DNA_curve_types.h	BKE_curve.h
DNA_curveprofile_types.h	BKE_curveprofile.h
DNA_customdata_types.h	BKE_customdata.h
DNA_dynamicpaint_types.h	BKE_dynamicpaint.h
DNA_effect_types.h	BKE_effect.h
DNA_fluid_types.h	BKE_fluid.h
DNA_freestyle_types.h	BKE_freestyle.h
DNA_gpencil_types.h	BKE_gpencil.h
DNA_image_types.h	BKE_image.h
DNA_ipo_types.h	BKE_ipo.h
DNA_key_types.h	BKE_key.h
DNA_lattice_types.h	BKE_lattice.h
DNA_layer_types.h	BKE_layer.h
DNA_light_types.h	BKE_light.h
DNA_lightprobe_types.h	BKE_lightprobe.h
DNA_linestyle_types.h	BKE_linestyle.h
DNA_mask_types.h	BKE_mask.h
DNA_material_types.h	BKE_material.h
DNA_mesh_types.h	BKE_mesh.h
DNA_modifier_types.h	BKE_modifier.h
DNA_movieclip_types.h	BKE_movieclip.h
DNA_nla_types.h	BKE_nla.h
DNA_node_types.h	BKE_node.h
DNA_object_types.h	BKE_object.h
DNA_outliner_types.h	BKE_outliner_treehash.h

(*continued*)

Table 4-1. (*continued*)

makesdna File	blenkernel File
DNA_packedFile_types.h	BKE_packedFile.h
DNA_particle_types.h	BKE_particle.h
DNA_rigidbody_types.h	BKE_rigidbody.h
DNA_scene_types.h	BKE_scene.h
DNA_screen_types.h	BKE_screen.h
DNA_sequence_types.h	BKE_sequencer.h
DNA_shader_fx_types.h	BKE_shader_fx.h
DNA_sound_types.h	BKE_sound.h
DNA_speaker_types.h	BKE_speaker.h
DNA_text_types.h	BKE_text.h
DNA_texture_types.h	BKE_texture.h
DNA_tracking_types.h	BKE_tracking.h
DNA_world_types.h	BKE_world.h

blenkernel API Examples

BKE_world.h

The following examples are illustrative of blenkernel's API for "DNA."

The BKE_* module API functions prototyped in *BKE_world.h* are shown in Listing 4-10.

Listing 4-10. Example BKE_world.h API prototypes. Function names are in boldface

```
...
void BKE_world_free(struct World *sc);
void BKE_world_init(struct World *wrld);
struct World *BKE_world_add(struct Main *bmain, const char *name);
```

```
void BKE_world_copy_data(struct Main *bmain,
                         struct World *wrld_dst,
                         const struct World *wrld_src,
                         const int flag);
struct World *BKE_world_copy(struct Main *bmain, const struct
World *wrld);
struct World *BKE_world_localize(struct World *wrld);
void BKE_world_make_local(struct Main *bmain, struct World
*wrld, const bool lib_local);
void BKE_world_eval(struct Depsgraph *depsgraph, struct World
*world);
...
```

BKE_camera.h

The BKE_* module API functions prototyped in *BKE_camera.h* are shown in Listing 4-11.

Listing 4-11. Example BKE_camera.h API prototypes. Function names are in boldface

```
...
/* Camera Datablock */

void BKE_camera_init(struct Camera *cam);
void *BKE_camera_add(struct Main *bmain, const char *name);
void BKE_camera_copy_data(struct Main *bmain,
                          struct Camera *cam_dst,
                          const struct Camera *cam_src,
                          const int flag);
struct Camera *BKE_camera_copy(struct Main *bmain, const struct
Camera *cam);
```

```
void BKE_camera_make_local(struct Main *bmain, struct Camera
*cam, const bool lib_local);
void BKE_camera_free(struct Camera *ca);

/* Camera Usage */

float BKE_camera_object_dof_distance(struct Object *ob);

int BKE_camera_sensor_fit(int sensor_fit, float sizex, float
sizey);
float BKE_camera_sensor_size(int sensor_fit, float sensor_x,
float sensor_y);
...
```

As we have discussed, blenkernel provides functions for operating on various Blender objects. Importantly, not all of these objects originate in makesdna. Two prominent examples, struct Main and struct bContext, are in fact defined in blenkernel itself. Note that struct Main and struct bContext are only two examples. Other types fit this pattern as well, such as struct Global.

BKE_main.h

The BKE_* module API functions prototyped in *BKE_main.h* are shown in Listing 4-12. struct Main is defined in *BKE_main.h*. The file *source/blender/blenkernel/intern/main.c* implements the related API.

Listing 4-12. Example BKE_main.h API prototypes. Function names are in boldface

```
...
struct Main *BKE_main_new(void);
void BKE_main_free(struct Main *mainvar);

void BKE_main_lock(struct Main *bmain);
void BKE_main_unlock(struct Main *bmain);
```

```
void BKE_main_relations_create(struct Main *bmain, const short
flag);
void BKE_main_relations_free(struct Main *bmain);

struct GSet *BKE_main_gset_create(struct Main *bmain, struct
GSet *gset);
```

...

BKE_context.h

The BKE_* module API functions prototyped in *BKE_context.h* are shown in Listing 4-13. struct bContext is defined in *source/blender/blenkernel/intern/context.c*. Related functions are also defined in *context.c*.

Listing 4-13. Example BKE_context.h API prototypes. Function names are in boldface

```
...
/* Context */

bContext *CTX_create(void);
void CTX_free(bContext *C);

bContext *CTX_copy(const bContext *C);

/* Stored Context */

bContextStore *CTX_store_add(ListBase *contexts, const char
*name, PointerRNA *ptr);
bContextStore *CTX_store_add_all(ListBase *contexts,
bContextStore *context);
void CTX_store_set(bContext *C, bContextStore *store);
bContextStore *CTX_store_copy(bContextStore *store);
void CTX_store_free(bContextStore *store);
void CTX_store_free_list(ListBase *contexts);
```

```
/* need to store if python is initialized or not */
bool CTX_py_init_get(bContext *C);
void CTX_py_init_set(bContext *C, bool value);

void *CTX_py_dict_get(const bContext *C);
void CTX_py_dict_set(bContext *C, void *value);
...
```

Summary

In this chapter, we looked at the blenlib and blenkernel modules. We also saw some of Blender's unit tests, which are helpful in understanding parts of the codebase. Blender uses Google Test for at least some of its testing.

blendlib handles generic utilities in Blender, while blenkernel is more specific to the Blender application. Therefore, blenlib's functionality, at least in principle, could be used by other similar programs. However, blenlib is tightly coupled to the Blender codebase— more so than, say GHOST, which is not part of the "core" codebase as we saw in Chapter 3.

blenkernel, on the other hand, offers a number of API functions for making needed manipulations on Blender "DNA," and other state-keeping data structures. We provided a list of the correspondence between makesdna and blenkernel's files, to illustrate the partial pairing of those modules.

CHAPTER 5

Blender's Embedded Python

CPython is a C-based implementation of Python. It even contains an API. This allows CPython to be used as an external library and linked with a separate application written in C. Functions defined by an "embedding" program may be called via Python script, running on the embedded interpreter. As such, Blender itself embeds a Python interpreter, providing access to some of its own functions. Python-callable functions must be registered using the Python API. This is done by Blender's python module.

The Blender python Module

Blender makes use of Python in multiple ways. One focus in this chapter is the python module and how its code calls the interpreter. We also look at function registration for the mathutils Python API module.

Because Python is object-oriented, Blender creates "built-in" Python modules and classes, some of whose methods map to Blender's internal C structs (as in the case of struct bContext) and internal module APIs, for example, the bmesh module. mathutils's mathematical objects, such as vectors and matrices, are assigned a Python class. Math utility functions from blenlib become methods for these same Python classes.

© Brad E. Hollister 2021
B. E. Hollister, *Core Blender Development*,
https://doi.org/10.1007/978-1-4842-6415-7_5

Source Files and Directories

Top-level directory contents for the python module are shown in Figure 5-1. We see in Figure 5-2 the internal and external dependencies for subdirectories in the python module.

Figure 5-1. *Top-level directory in the python module. rna_dump.py and simple_enum_gen.py generate C source code. In simple_enum_gen.py, you can see calls that generate* PyModule_AddObject(), *a Python API function.* BPY_extern.h *supplies prototypes for the python module API.* BPY_extern_clog.h *is used for logging*

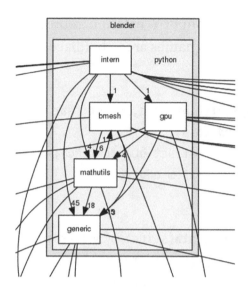

Figure 5-2. *Partial dependency graph for the subdirectories of the python module. Arrows point in the direction of the dependency*

The python module provides a Python API for parts of the codebase. There are internal dependencies between subdirectories as well. One salient example is *source/blender/python/intern*'s dependency on *source/blender/python/generic/*.

The python module API

The python module API prototypes are provided by *source/blender/python/BPY_extern.h*. As with other modules, the API is called either inside or outside of the module. A sample of the BPY_* functions is shown in Listing 5-1.

Both BPY_python_start() and BPY_python_end() are called from windowmanager, during both initialization and shutdown. Other prominent API functions execute Python script, usually as the result of an operator's callback function. BPY_execute_filepath(), BPY_execute_text(), and BPY_execute_string_as_number() each invoke the interpreter.

Listing 5-1. Snippet from BPY_extern.h, representing part of the module's API. Function names are in boldface

...

```
void BPY_python_start(int argc, const char **argv);
void BPY_python_end(void);
void BPY_python_reset(struct bContext *C);
void BPY_python_use_system_env(void);
```

...

```
bool BPY_execute_filepath(struct bContext *C, const char
*filepath, struct ReportList *reports);
bool BPY_execute_text(struct bContext *C,
                      struct Text *text,
                      struct ReportList *reports,
                      const bool do_jump);

bool BPY_execute_string_as_number(struct bContext *C,
                                  const char *imports[],
                                  const char *expr,
                                  const bool verbose,
                                  double *r_value);
```

...

Extending and Embedding Python

Before we go into the mechanics of the python module, we need to understand how to run the Python interpreter using the CPython API. Python's primary documentation related to this is "Embedding

Python in Another Application."[1] Most of this information can be distilled to just a number of steps.

Note that CPython API prototypes are in *Python.h*. A program using the CPython API must contain the preprocessor directive #include <Python. h>, assuming Python is in the system path.

When building Blender, there is a CMake variable that can be set to use the Python installation or to download binaries to be placed in the build directory under *[build directory]/bin/share/blender/[Blender version]/ python/*.

Adding Python Extensions

Let us take a look at the CPython API and a few related structs. These also happen to be the CPython API functions Blender's codebase uses most, although there are variants in some cases. First, we present the CPython API for creating extensions:

- PyModule_New()

- PyModule_Create()

- PyModule_AddObject()

- PyImport_ExtendInittab()

PyModule_New() and PyModule_Create() both are used to add an extension module. For instance, Blender's Python mathutils module is added by PyModule_Create(), while its bpy module is via PyModule_New(). PyModule_New() was introduced in version 3.3 of the CPython, after PyModule_Create(). You will see both functions used for creating new modules in Blender.

---

[1]At the time of this publication, Python 3.7 is the bundled version with Blender 2.83. The corresponding python.org documentation is https://docs.python. org/3.7/extending/embedding.html.

`PyModule_AddObject()` adds a class to a module. For example, the `mathutils.Vector` is added as a built-in Python class using `PyModule_AddObject()`. `PyImport_ExtendInittab()` registers modules to be included in Python's initialization table (i.e., `Inittab` from the function name). This table contains extension modules to be registered when Python is initialized.

The C `structs` in the CPython API related to extensions are

- `PyObject`

- `PyTypeObject`

- `PyMethodDef`

- `PyModuleDef`

- `PyCFunction`

All Python objects are "derived" from `PyObject`. `PyObject` `structs` are "extended," by adding `PyObject_HEAD` to a user-defined `struct`.

Note   In C, there is no explicit language mechanism for inheritance. By adding common fields to the beginning of a user-defined `struct`, we can treat these `structs` as having inherited those fields. In CPython, user-defined `structs` starting with `PyObject_HEAD` are treated as objects with the base type `PyObject`. We saw an example of this in Chapter 2, for "DNA" types. There, the `ID` `struct` is placed at the beginning of each "DNA" type. This method of "inheritance" is used extensively in Blender's codebase.

PyObject_HEAD is expanded by the preprocessor into two fields. One field points to an object of PyTypeObject, the other a count of the object's references.[2]

PyTypeObject contains, in addition to function pointers for an object's type, a PyVarObject_HEAD_INIT macro similar to PyObject_HEAD. PyTypeObject also has a field for a PyObject's size.

Some Python methods, for example, __init__(), are added as fields to a PyTypeObject, the one using it as its type definition. Other types of methods must be added to a PyMethodDef object. The PyTypeObject.tb_methods field points to a methods table (an object of type PyMethodDef). Note that there is a separate PyGetSetDef methods table, used extensively in the implementation of the mathutils.Vector class.

PyModuleDef is used when defining a Python extension module. mathutils's submodules contain functions. Its function registration uses PyModuleDef. However, registration for functions still looks quite similar to the use of PyMethodDef. PyModuleDef and PyMethodDef are shown in Listing 5-2.

Listing 5-2. The PyMethodDef and PyModuleDef objects of the mathutils extension module (source/blender/python/mathutils/mathutils.c). mathutils does not contain functions defined in the mathutils namespace alone. All functionality is attached to its various classes or functions in its submodules (geometry, bvhtree, etc.)

```
static struct PyMethodDef M_Mathutils_methods[] = {
    {NULL, NULL, 0, NULL},
};
```

---

[2]You will see reference counting used in the methods added as part of Blender's extended Python for Blender. The CPython API functions Py_INCREF() and Py_DECREF() are used for counting PyObject references.

```
static struct PyModuleDef M_Mathutils_module_def = {
    PyModuleDef_HEAD_INIT,
    "mathutils",            /* m_name */
    M_Mathutils_doc,        /* m_doc */
    0,                      /* m_size */
    M_Mathutils_methods,    /* m_methods */
    NULL,                   /* m_reload */
    NULL,                   /* m_traverse */
    NULL,                   /* m_clear */
    NULL,                   /* m_free */
};
```

The CPython API functions for embedding and running Python are

- `Py_Initialize()`

- `Py_Finalize()`

- `PyEval_EvalCode()`

`Py_Intialize()` is called to initialize the Python interpreter before any module registration. This is done after a call to `PyImport_ExtendInittab()`, where the list of built-in modules are added (see Listing 5-3). `Py_Finalize()` is called from `BPY_python_end()`, which is invoked outside of the `python` module, during shutdown. `PyEval_EvalCode()` is called when an entire script (text file) is loaded and run, or as text from the Blender script editor. Python code executed from the interactive console editor runs by a call generated by the Python library itself.

Listing 5-3. Abbreviated initialization table in source/blender/python/intern/bpy_interface.c. This table is used to add extensions to the list of "built-in" modules, before a call to `Py_Initialize()`. Each entry in `bpy_internal_modules` is `structs`, with an identifier for the module and a function pointer to the initialization function

PyMODINIT_FUNC. Each of these modules is then initialized with member classes, functions, etc

```
static struct _inittab bpy_internal_modules[] = {
    {"mathutils", PyInit_mathutils},
#if 0
    {"mathutils.geometry", PyInit_mathutils_geometry},
    {"mathutils.noise", PyInit_mathutils_noise},
    {"mathutils.kdtree", PyInit_mathutils_kdtree},
#endif
    {"_bpy_path", BPyInit__bpy_path},
    {"bgl", BPyInit_bgl},
    {"blf", BPyInit_blf},
    {"imbuf", BPyInit_imbuf},
    {"bmesh", BPyInit_bmesh},
...
};
```

BPY_execute_filepath() and BPY_execute_text() both call PyEval_EvalCode(), which in turn calls python_script_exec(). python_script_exec() is defined in *source/blender/python/intern/bpy_interface.c*. If the script has not already been compiled, then Py_CompileStringObject() is first executed. The resulting Python bytecode is placed in Text's compiled field. *source/blender/python/bpy.c* and *source/blender/python/bpy_interface.c* (among others) make extensive use of the CPython API.

The mathutils Extension Module

As mentioned, one of the Blender Python extension modules is mathutils. It has fewer dependencies than other extensions. Additionally, it does not involve Blender "RNA," as can be seen in its dependency graph of Figure 5-3.

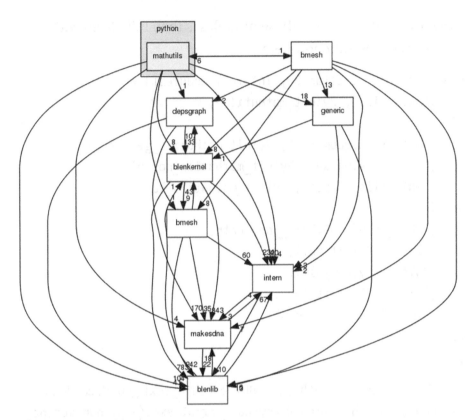

Figure 5-3. *Dependencies of source/blender/python/mathutils/. There are separate* bmesh *nodes in the graph. The red* bmesh *node represents the external dependency source/blender/bmesh/. The black* bmesh *node represents source/blender/python/bmesh/, a dependency within the python module*

Blender "RNA" is covered in Chapter 6. Figure 5-4 shows the file contents of *source/blender/python/mathutils/*.

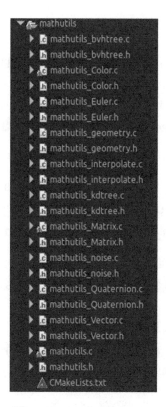

Figure 5-4. *The* mathutils *directory from the python module. The directory contains the implementation of the* mathutils *Python module.* mathutils *features math utilities representing objects such as vectors, matrices, and quaternions*

Implementation of the `mathutils.Vector` Class

In this section, we go over the implementation of the mathutils.Vector Python class. It is a good example to illustrate how Blender implements an extension module's class.

VectorObject

As mentioned, newly "built-in" classes are derived from the PyObject struct. This is done by including a header at the start of the struct definition. For the mathutils module, Blender uses BASE_MATH_MEMBERS (see Listing 5-4), which contains the PyObject_HEAD macro from the CPython API.

Listing 5-4. The BASE_MATH_MEMBERS macro (defined in source/ blender/python/mathutils/mathutils.h). PyObject_VAR_HEAD is included in BASE_MATH_MEMBERS, and shown in boldface

```
#define BASE_MATH_MEMBERS(_data) \
  /** Array of data (alias), wrapped status depends on wrapped
  status. */ \
  PyObject_VAR_HEAD float *_data; \
  /** If this vector references another object, otherwise NULL,
  *Note* this owns its reference */ \
  PyObject *cb_user; \
  /** Which user funcs do we adhere to, RNA, etc */ \
  unsigned char cb_type; \
  /** Subtype: location, rotation... \
   * to avoid defining many new functions for every attribute
    of the same type */ \
  unsigned char cb_subtype; \
  /** Wrapped data type. */ \
  unsigned char flag
```

mathutils.Vector is represented by VectorObject, shown in Listing 5-5. It uses BASE_MATH_MEMBERS as described. Notice also that VectorObject contains an instance variable size.

Listing 5-5. The VectorObject struct. This is the "derived" PyObject for mathutils.Vector. BASE_MATH_MEMBERS is shown in boldface

```
typedef struct {
  BASE_MATH_MEMBERS(vec);

  int size; /* vec size 2 or more */
} VectorObject;
```

Adding Methods to **vector_Type**

For mathutils.Vector, the methods are referenced by the tp_methods field. The PyTypeObject for mathutils.Vector is vector_Type (Listing 5-6). Instead, vector_Type uses PyGetSetDef, defined in *source/blender/python/mathutils/mathutils_Vector.c*. It assigns tp_getset an array of PyGetSetDef objects, one for each getter and setter method pair.

Listing 5-6. The vector_Type definition for mathutils.Vector. tp_alloc is NULL. This is significant because Vector_new() must allocate a VectorObject. Since tp_alloc is NULL, a call will be made to _PyObject_GC_New()—a CPython API function—using the BASE_MATH_NEW macro

```
PyTypeObject vector_Type = {
    PyVarObject_HEAD_INIT(NULL, 0)
    /* For printing, in format "<module>.<name>" */
    "Vector",                /* char *tp_name; */
...

    /*** Attribute descriptor and subclassing stuff ***/
    Vector_methods,    /* struct PyMethodDef *tp_methods; */
    NULL,              /* struct PyMemberDef *tp_members; */
```

```
    Vector_getseters, /* struct PyGetSetDef *tp_getset; */
...
    NULL,              /* allocfunc tp_alloc; */
    Vector_new,        /* newfunc tp_new; */
...
};
```

This implementation allows a getter method to return a value representing the length of the vector, instead of providing direct access to size. mathutils.Vector.length() is the associated getter and is registered in the PyGetSetDef object definition as follows:

```
{"length", (getter)Vector_length_get, (setter)Vector_length_
set, Vector_length_doc, NULL}
```

The C functions that implement the getter and setter are Vector_length_get and Vector_length_set, respectively. The struct also contains the Python docstring, displayed when the Python's built-in help() is called in a script. The last field of the PyGetSetDef struct is left NULL, as it is the optional closure slot.

Vector_new()'s Implementation

It will aid in our understanding of mathutils.Vector, to see how instances of this Python class are allocated. From Listing 5-6, we saw that the tp_new slot of vector_Type points to Vector_new(). Vector_new() is responsible for the top-level allocation of an instance of mathutils.Vector. A snippet of Vector_new() C function is shown in Listing 5-7.

Listing 5-7. Abbreviated Vector_new() from python/mathutils/ mathutils_Vector.c. Vector_new() creates VectorObjects. Notice that it calls blenlib's math utility copy_vn_fl(), shown in boldface

```
static PyObject *Vector_new(PyTypeObject *type, PyObject *args,
PyObject *kwds)
{
  float *vec = NULL;
  int size = 3; /* default to a 3D vector */
...
  switch (PyTuple_GET_SIZE(args)) {
    case 0:
      vec = PyMem_Malloc(size * sizeof(float));
...
      copy_vn_fl(vec, size, 0.0f);
      break;
...

  }
  return Vector_CreatePyObject_alloc(vec, size, type);
}
```

Once called, Vector_new() assigns its local variable vec, to a dynamically allocated array of floats via PyMem_Malloc(). The allocation uses the CPython API, not Blender's *intern/guardedalloc* library (see Chapter 1).

From there, Vector_new() calls copy_vn_fl(). The copy_vn_fl() function initializes a "zero" memory copy to vec. See Listing 5-8 for the copy_vn_fl() source. It is important to realize that not all Blender Python extensions use blenlib. In fact, Blender Python extension modules have dependencies on Blender "RNA" and the associated Data API.

Listing 5-8. copy_vn_fl() from source/blender/blenlib/intern/
math_vector.c. The function starts at the last component of the
array and decrements the tar pointer down to the first entry of vec,
assigning each entry with the parameter val

```
void copy_vn_fl(float *array_tar, const int size, const float val)
{
  float *tar = array_tar + (size - 1);
  int i = size;
  while (i--) {
    *(tar--) = val;
  }
}
```

After copy_vn_fl() initializes vec, the data portion of a mathutils.
Vector object, Vector_new() calls Vector_CreatePyObject_alloc().
Looking at Listing 5-9, we see that there is more than one function for
creating a VectorObject.

Listing 5-9. source/blender/python/mathutils/mathutils_Vector.h's
prototypes for instantiating VectorObjects. These are used for a
copy constructor, swizzling operators, etc. source/blender/python/
mathutils/mathutils_Vector.c contains the function definitions

```
/*prototypes*/
PyObject *Vector_CreatePyObject(const float *vec,
                                const int size,
                                PyTypeObject *base_type) ATTR_
                                WARN_UNUSED_RESULT;
PyObject *Vector_CreatePyObject_wrap(float *vec,
                                const int size,
                                PyTypeObject *base_type)
                                ATTR_WARN_UNUSED_RESULT
```

```
    ATTR_NONNULL(1);
PyObject *Vector_CreatePyObject_cb(PyObject *user,
                                   int size,
                                   unsigned char cb_type,
                                   unsigned char subtype) ATTR_
                                   WARN_UNUSED_RESULT;
PyObject *Vector_CreatePyObject_alloc(float *vec,
                                      const int size,
                                      PyTypeObject *base_type)
                                      ATTR_WARN_UNUSED_RESULT
    ATTR_NONNULL(1);
```

Since we start with a float array in Vector_new(), Vector_
CreatePyObject_alloc()'s responsibility is to use the float array data and
wrap it in a PyObject, which in this case is the derived PyObject of type
VectorObject. A PyObject representation of a Python class instance is its C
side equivalent. As such, a copy of VectorObject, pointing to its associated
data (i.e., its float array) is required. Py_CreatePyObject_alloc() calls
Vector_CreatePyObject_wrap(), as shown in Listing 5-10.

Listing 5-10. Vector_CreatePyObject_alloc() and an abbreviated
Vector_CreatePyObject_wrap(). Subsequent calls for allocation are
in boldface

```
PyObject *Vector_CreatePyObject_alloc(float *vec, const int
size, PyTypeObject *base_type)
{
  VectorObject *self;
  self = (VectorObject *)Vector_CreatePyObject_wrap(vec, size,
  base_type);
  if (self) {
    self->flag &= ~BASE_MATH_FLAG_IS_WRAP;
  }
```

```
  return (PyObject *)self;
}

PyObject *Vector_CreatePyObject_wrap(float *vec, const int
size, PyTypeObject *base_type)
{
  VectorObject *self;
...
  self = BASE_MATH_NEW(VectorObject, vector_Type, base_type);
...
  return (PyObject *)self;
}
```

Vector_CreatePyObject_wrap() uses BASE_MATH_NEW (see Listing 5-11), due to the absence of a tp_alloc method in the VectorTypeObject for mathtutils.Vector. Vector_CreatePyObject_wrap() must call a CPython memory allocator for the VectorObject itself.

Listing 5-11. The BASE_MATH_NEW macro defined in source/blender/python/mathutils/mathutils.h. BASE_MATH_NEW issues a call to either the tp_alloc method or _PyObject_GC_New(), a CPython function

```
#define BASE_MATH_NEW(struct_name, root_type, base_type) \
  ((struct_name *)((base_type ? (base_type)->tp_alloc(base_
  type, 0) : \
                            _PyObject_GC_New(&(root_
                            type)))))
```

Exploration of other extension classes and __new__() method implementations reveal differences with Vector_new(). mathutils. Vector is not tied to a Blender "DNA" type. Extension classes that have corresponding "DNA" are likely to use Blender "RNA."

Vector_normalize()'s Implementation

We now have an example of a "non-magic" method from the `mathtutils`.
Vector class, `mathutils.Vector.normalize()`. `mathutils.Vector`.
`normalize()`'s implementation is the definition for `Vector_normalize()`,
seen in Listing 5-12.

Listing 5-12. The `PyMethodDef` for `Vector.normalize()`

```
static struct PyMethodDef Vector_methods[] = {
    /* Class Methods */
    {"Fill", (PyCFunction)C_Vector_Fill, METH_VARARGS | METH_
    CLASS, C_Vector_Fill_doc},
...
    /* operate on original or copy */
    {"normalize", (PyCFunction)Vector_normalize, METH_NOARGS,
    Vector_normalize_doc},
...
    {NULL, NULL, 0, NULL},
};
```

`Vector_normalize()` is called by the interpreter, whenever an instance
of the `mathutils.Vector` class invokes its `normalize()` method. It takes
a pointer to a `VectorObject` containing vector entries (a float array).
`Vector_normalize()` must call `blenlib`'s `normalize_vn()` to do the raw
mathematical work of normalizing a vector (see Listing 5-13).[3]

---

[3]Incidentally, there is also a call to `BaseMath_WriteCallback()` in `Vector_`
`normalize()`. Each `PyObject` subtype in `mathutils` may have a callback function.
Callbacks are used by `mathutils.Matrix` (in `MatrixObject`) and implemented
in functions with the suffix `*_cb`. The `Vector_CreatePyObject_cb()` allocation
function, from *mathutils_Vector.c*, allocates a `mathutils.Vector` instance when
the callback is invoked.

Listing 5-13. Vector_normalize(), which defines the Python extension method Vector.normalize(). The blendlib function normalize_vn() is in boldface

```
static PyObject *Vector_normalize(VectorObject *self)
{
  int size = (self->size == 4 ? 3 : self->size);
  if (BaseMath_ReadCallback_ForWrite(self) == -1) {
    return NULL;
  }

  normalize_vn(self->vec, size);

  (void)BaseMath_WriteCallback(self);
  Py_RETURN_NONE;
}
```

Other mathutils.Vector Methods

There are many methods from mathutils.Vector in addition to the ones described. A good place to start is with the PyMethodDef array from *source/blender/python/mathutils/mathutils_Vector.c* (Listing 5-14). The PyCFunction type cast designates a C function. This function is called by the method name, in the first field of PyMethodDef. For instance, mathutils.Vector.Fill() is implemented by C_Vector_Fill(), as shown in Vector_methods[].[4] The termination of a methods table is done with a "sentinel," a NULL-data containing entry. The sentinel here is {NULL, NULL, 0, NULL}, a "nulled out" PyMethodDef struct.

---

[4]Class methods of mathutils.Vector, i.e., ones that can be called without an instance of the mathutils.Vector class (known as static member functions in C++), have C_* prepended to their identifiers. Python class methods may update class state, but not object state.

Listing 5-14. Abbreviated Vector_methods[] from mathutils_ Vector.c. The sentinel and the "Fill" method registration are both shown in boldface

```
static struct PyMethodDef Vector_methods[] = {
    /* Class Methods */
    {"Fill", (PyCFunction)C_Vector_Fill, METH_VARARGS |
    METH_CLASS, C_Vector_Fill_doc},
    {"Range", (PyCFunction)C_Vector_Range,
...

    /* operate on original or copy */
    {"normalize", (PyCFunction)Vector_normalize, METH_NOARGS,
    Vector_normalize_doc},
    {"normalized", (PyCFunction)Vector_normalized, METH_NOARGS,
    Vector_normalized_doc},
...

    /* operation between 2 or more types   */
    {"reflect", (PyCFunction)Vector_reflect, METH_O, Vector_
    reflect_doc},
    {"cross", (PyCFunction)Vector_cross, METH_O,
...

    /* base-math methods */
    {"freeze", (PyCFunction)BaseMathObject_freeze, METH_NOARGS,
    BaseMathObject_freeze_doc},
...

    {NULL, NULL, 0, NULL},
};
```

Submodules in `mathutils`

In Listing 5-15, we can see other classes defined in the Blender python module. Some of these include `mathutils.Quanterion`, `mathutils.Matrix`, and `mathutils.Color`.

Listing 5-15. Example of the `mathutils.noise` submodule initialization and function registration (from source/blender/python/mathutils/mathutils_noise.c). The submodule initialization function is `PyInit_mathutils_noise()`, shown in boldface. `M_Noise_methods[]` is abbreviated for brevity

```
static PyMethodDef M_Noise_methods[] = {
    {"seed_set", (PyCFunction)M_Noise_seed_set, METH_VARARGS,
    M_Noise_seed_set_doc},
    {"random", (PyCFunction)M_Noise_random,
...
    {"cell", (PyCFunction)M_Noise_cell, METH_VARARGS,
    M_Noise_cell_doc},
    {"cell_vector", (PyCFunction)M_Noise_cell_vector,
    METH_VARARGS, M_Noise_cell_vector_doc},
    {NULL, NULL, 0, NULL},
};

static struct PyModuleDef M_Noise_module_def = {
    PyModuleDef_HEAD_INIT,
    "mathutils.noise", /* m_name */
    M_Noise_doc,       /* m_doc */
    0,                 /* m_size */
    M_Noise_methods,   /* m_methods */
    NULL,              /* m_reload */
    NULL,              /* m_traverse */
    NULL,              /* m_clear */
```

```
    NULL,                    /* m_free */
};

/*-------------------------MODULE INIT---------------------
---*/
PyMODINIT_FUNC PyInit_mathutils_noise(void)
{
  PyObject *submodule = PyModule_Create(&M_Noise_module_def);

  /* use current time as seed for random number generator by
  default */
  setRndSeed(0);

  return submodule;
}
```

Files such as *mathutils_geometry.c* and *mathutils_noise.c* implement submodule functions (not methods). Without an associated class, their implementation requires less code. An example of this can be seen in *source/blender/python/mathutils/mathutils_noise.c*. M_Noise_module_def, a struct PyModuleDef, and its corresponding PyInit_mathutils_noise() function are added to bpy_internal_modules[] (Listing 5-16). We can see from bpy_internal_modules[] that creating submodules is no different from top-level modules. BPy_init_modules() is implemented in *source/blender/python/intern/bpy.c*. It is called after manual loading of all modules. This is where calls are made to PyModule_AddObject().

Listing 5-16. Abbreviated bpy_internal_modules[] and BPY_python_start() from source/blender/python/intern/bpy_interface.c

```
static struct _inittab bpy_internal_modules[] = {
    {"mathutils", PyInit_mathutils},
```

```
#if 0
    {"mathutils.geometry", PyInit_mathutils_geometry},
    {"mathutils.noise", PyInit_mathutils_noise},
    {"mathutils.kdtree", PyInit_mathutils_kdtree},
#endif
    {"_bpy_path", BPyInit__bpy_path},
    {"bgl", BPyInit_bgl},
    {"blf", BPyInit_blf},
    {"imbuf", BPyInit_imbuf},
    {"bmesh", BPyInit_bmesh},
#if 0
    {"bmesh.types", BPyInit_bmesh_types},
    {"bmesh.utils", BPyInit_bmesh_utils},
    {"bmesh.utils", BPyInit_bmesh_geometry},
#endif
...

    {NULL, NULL},
};
/* call BPY_context_set first */
void BPY_python_start(int argc, const char **argv)
{
...
  /* must run before python initializes */
  PyImport_ExtendInittab(bpy_internal_modules);

...

  Py_Initialize();

...
```

```c
#ifdef WITH_PYTHON_MODULE
  {
    /* Manually load all modules */
    struct _inittab *inittab_item;
    PyObject *sys_modules = PyImport_GetModuleDict();

    for (inittab_item = bpy_internal_modules; inittab_item-
    >name; inittab_item++) {
      PyObject *mod = inittab_item->initfunc();
      if (mod) {
        PyDict_SetItemString(sys_modules, inittab_item->name,
        mod);
      }
...
  }
#endif

  /* bpy.* and lets us import it */
  BPy_init_modules();
...

}
```

Summary

In this chapter, we discussed many of the fundamentals of Python extension, as handled in the python module. However, we did not discuss issues related to multithreading, while running the Python interpreter. A mutual exclusion lock (mutex) is necessary, so that the CPython library obtains the "global interpreter lock" (GIL), when working with shared PyObjects. This ensures that PyObjects are not updated by more than one running interpreter. The GIL is managed by various functions of the CPython API.

The python module also uses the CPython API to provide extensions to the Python interpreter. These extensions can be called from a Python script executed by Blender. We saw key parts of mathutils.Vector's implementation in Blender's codebase and how C functions are called when a script invokes mathutils.Vector's methods. This process is similar for all Blender Python extension classes.

CHAPTER 6

Blender "RNA" and the Data API

Blender "DNA" was described by example in Chapter 2, when we talked about Blender state and serialization. This chapter covers how the Blender codebase sets "DNA" variables via "RNA" properties.[1]

An additional aspect to the makesrna module is that multiple source files are generated during the build process. They are then fed back into the source code compiled as the runtime Blender executable. This means that makesrna is distinct from other Blender modules. It is implemented in this way, so that objects of "RNA" properties, that is, structs definitions with property data values such as initial settings, value ranges, and accessor function pointers, are not hand-coded. The makesrna module allows Blender developers to incorporate new "DNA" types by adding required wrapper code. In addition, a paradigm of the codebase is to

---

[1]Actual RNA (ribonucleic acid) is a biological molecule. It transcribes literal DNA (a separate molecule named deoxyribonucleic acid) by encoding (transcribing) it and then translating its encoding to protein. This process is known as the "central dogma of molecular biology." However, the protein aspect is where this analogy ends. Blender's "RNA" is essentially an interface to Blender's "DNA" types. Blender "RNA" also moves information (settings) into Blender "DNA," making Blender "RNA" capable of "reverse transcription" as well—i.e., an analogy to when information flows from RNA to DNA in biological systems.

© Brad E. Hollister 2021
B. E. Hollister, *Core Blender Development*,
https://doi.org/10.1007/978-1-4842-6415-7_6

"bake-in" elements of data, for runtime efficiency. This was another design consideration of the makesrna module, taking its direction from makesdna. However, makedna uses code generation to a lesser extent than makesrna, as will be seen.

The Blender makesrna Module

makesrna is somewhat non-standard in the Blender codebase. We explore its various parts, in the next few sections. There is a distinction between the Data API and the broader makesrna module API. As usual, the makerna API function names start with an RNA_* prefix.

Note   Some RNA_* functions are used more by non-runtime portions of the makesrna module for generating Data API backend functions (generated makesrna source code). The Data API RNA_* interface is provided in *[repository root]/source/blender/makesrna/ RNA_access.h*, whereas the makesrna RNA_* API interface, used heavily by the non-runtime makesrna code, is contained in *[repository root]/source/blender/makesrna/RNA_define.h.*

Runtime vs. Non-runtime Code

The makesrna module has both a runtime and non-runtime portion. The non-runtime portion is dedicated to source code generation.

An individual file in the repository's makesrna module may include both runtime and non-runtime code. Runtime code becomes part of the Blender executable. Non-runtime code is compiled as part of the tools that generate runtime code.

Note   This chapter references generated files which are created by a build and written to the build directory. Therefore, we preface each path with either *[repository root]* or *[build root]*.

During the build process, the makesrna program is run. It is compiled from *[repository root]/source/blender/makesrna/intern/makesrna.c*. *makesrna.c* contains no runtime code. Many of the files in *[repository root]/source/blender/makesrna/intern/* have a separate runtime and non-runtime portion that is included (or excluded) from compilation by the preprocessor.

At the top of every generated source file is the macro #define RNA_ RUNTIME. The source code in generated files belongs to the runtime. By defining the RNA_RUNTIME macro, the generated files affect which part of a repository source file is compiled. As such, many of the source files in the repository are compiled twice, first for the non-runtime and then for the runtime after RNA_RUNTIME is defined by the generated source.

Repository "RNA" Code

We will look at the makesrna module's generated code, after first inspecting the repository's "RNA" code. Figure 6-1 shows the repository's makesrna module top-level directory.

The primary source files in the top-level directory of the makesrna are *RNA_types.h*, *RNA_enum_types.h*, *RNA_access.h*, and *RNA_define.h*.[2] This layout is similar to many Blender modules, in that there is an *intern* subdirectory containing the implementation of the module's API and functions used internally by the module itself.

---

[2]The official documentation (https://wiki.blender.org/wiki/Source/ Architecture/RNA) provides information on the design consideration for "RNA," at the time of Blender 2.5 development. When the document was written, the file contents were fewer, and the generated code was written to a single file.

Figure 6-1. *The* makesrna *top-level directory contents*

RNA_types.h

"RNA" types used directly outside of makesrna are defined in *RNA_types.h*. For example, PointerRNA is used extensively in the python module. However, StructRNA is only used indirectly via the PointerRNA type and therefore defined in *[repository root]/source/blender/makesrna/intern/ rna_internal_types.h*.

RNA_enum_types.h

RNA_enum_types.h prototypes RNA_* API calls that return enumerations using EnumPropertyItem (Listing 6-1). It is not responsible for defining enums such as PropertyType, which are instead defined in *RNA_types.h*.

Listing 6-1. The EnumPropertyItem struct defined in RNA_types.h

```
/**
 * This struct is are typically defined in arrays which define
   an *enum* for RNA,
 * which is used by the RNA API both for user-interface and the
   Python API.
 */
```

```
typedef struct EnumPropertyItem {
  /** The internal value of the enum, not exposed to users. */
  int value;
  /**
    * Note that identifiers must be unique within the array,
    * by convention they're upper case with underscores for
      separators.
    * - An empty string is used to define menu separators.
    * - NULL denotes the end of the array of items.
    */
  const char *identifier;
  /** Optional icon, typically 'ICON_NONE' */
  int icon;
  /** Name displayed in the interface. */
  const char *name;
  /** Longer description used in the interface. */
  const char *description;
} EnumPropertyItem;
```

RNA_access.h

RNA_access.h contains prototypes for the runtime Data API. These functions allow access to properties held by a PointerRNA's StructRNA field. Example prototypes for property access to float data are shown in Listing 6-2. StructRNA has pointers to RNAProperty objects (e.g., FloatRNAProperty, IntRNAProperty, etc.). Property objects have accessors in the generated runtime files, comprising the Data API's backend.

Listing 6-2. Example of float property Data API accessors, prototyped in [repository root]/source/blender/makesrna/RNA_access.h

```
...
float RNA_property_float_get(PointerRNA *ptr, PropertyRNA
*prop);
void RNA_property_float_set(PointerRNA *ptr, PropertyRNA *prop,
float value);
void RNA_property_float_get_array(PointerRNA *ptr, PropertyRNA
*prop, float *values);
...
```

RNA_define.h

RNA_define.h is a set of function prototypes for creating instances of "RNA" structs used by both runtime and non-runtime portions of makesrna. These functions are named with an RNA_def_* prefix and implemented in *[repository root]/source/blender/makesrna/intern/rna_access.c*.

Client code of the prototyped API in *RNA_define.h* is a binary program compiled from *[repository root]/source/blender/makesrna/intern/ makesrna.c. makesrna.c* is analogous to *makesdna.c*, from Chapter 2. It is responsible for generating source files for the runtime Data API backend, for each "DNA" type.

The *intern* Subdirectory Contents

makesrna's *intern* subdirectory contains source files prefixed by *rna_**. There is an *rna_*.c* source file for every "DNA" type that is wrapped by "RNA." *rna_*_api.c* functions implement callbacks triggered when an object is updated by the Data API, usually in response to values changed in the user interface or Python API call via an operator.

There are two parts to these files, a runtime and a non-runtime portion. The runtime portion is used for additional Data API backend functionality not written to the generated source files. This code is responsible for "refine" functions. These functions return a StructRNA, which represents a "DNA" type refinement, for example, a point light.

The non-runtime calls RNA_def_* API, setting fields on either BlenderRNA or StructRNA objects for a "DNA" type. There is an upcoming example for the Light struct ("DNA") later in the chapter. That example will discuss *makesrna/intern/rna_light.c*.

"RNA" Types

There are two categories of "RNA." The first type is accessed only through the RNA_* API and implemented in *rna_internal_types.c*. The second type of "RNA" is defined in *RNA_types.h* and manipulated by functions defined outside of makesrna. For instance, PointerRNA is from *RNA_types.h* and therefore accessed by code external to makesrna—mostly in the python module. The following descriptions are of the main "RNA" types.

StructRNA

StructRNA is shown in Listing 6-3 and Figure 6-2. It is used for defining the properties on "RNA" wrappers of "DNA" type data.

Listing 6-3. StructRNA from rna_internal_types.h. Used in both the "RNA" runtime and makesrna.c

```
/* changes to this struct require updating rna_generate_struct
in makesrna.c */
struct StructRNA {
  /* structs are containers of properties */
  ContainerRNA cont;
```

```
/* unique identifier, keep after 'cont' */
const char *identifier;

/** Python type, this is a subtype of #pyrna_struct_Type
 * but used so each struct can have its own type which is
   useful for subclassing RNA. */
void *py_type;
void *blender_type;

/* various options */
int flag;
/* Each StructRNA type can define own tags which properties
   can set
 * (PropertyRNA.tags) for changed behavior based on
   struct-type. */
const EnumPropertyItem *prop_tag_defines;

/* user readable name */
const char *name;
/* single line description, displayed in the tooltip for
   example */
const char *description;
/* context for translation */
const char *translation_context;
/* icon ID */
int icon;

/* property that defines the name */
PropertyRNA *nameproperty;

/* property to iterate over properties */
PropertyRNA *iteratorproperty;
```

```
/* struct this is derivedfrom */
struct StructRNA *base;

/* only use for nested structs, where both the parent and
   child access
 * the same C Struct but nesting is used for grouping
   properties.
 * The parent property is used so we know NULL checks are not
   needed,
 * and that this struct will never exist without its parent
*/
struct StructRNA *nested;

/* function to give the more specific type */
StructRefineFunc refine;

/* function to find path to this struct in an ID */
StructPathFunc path;

/* function to register/unregister subclasses */
StructRegisterFunc reg;
StructUnregisterFunc unreg;
StructInstanceFunc instance;

/* callback to get id properties */
IDPropertiesFunc idproperties;

/* functions of this struct */
ListBase functions;
};
```

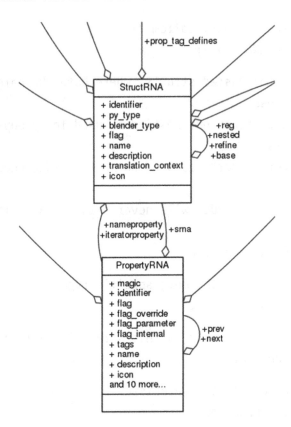

Figure 6-2. *Collaboration between* StructRNA *and* PropertyRNA *objects. Other aggregations are clipped*

Note   "RNA" is used to encapsulate information pertaining to "DNA," as used in operators for data definitions and settings.

StructRNA objects are written to the generated source. RNA_Light is one such StructRNA object. We can see its definition in Listing 6-4. Here, we can see values that populate the fields of StructRNA. Its accessor functions are defined in *rna_light.c* (repository code) and in the generated source file *rna_light_gen.c*.

Listing 6-4. RNA_Light definition from [build root]/source/blender/ makerna/intern/rna_light_gen.c. rna_Light_type is in boldface, as it is important for later discussion

```
StructRNA RNA_Light = {
    {(ContainerRNA *)&RNA_PointLight, (ContainerRNA *)&RNA_
    ShapeKeyBezierPoint,
    NULL,
    {(PropertyRNA *)&rna_Light_type, (PropertyRNA *)&rna_
    Light_animation_data}},
    "Light", NULL, NULL, 519, NULL, "Light",
    "Light data-block for lighting a scene",
    "Light", 164,
    (PropertyRNA *)&rna_ID_name, (PropertyRNA *)&rna_ID_rna_
    properties,
    &RNA_ID,
    NULL,
    rna_Light_refine,
    NULL,
    NULL,
    NULL,
    rna_ID_instance,
    rna_ID_idprops,
    {NULL, NULL}
};
```

ContainerRNA

As discussed, StructRNA and PropertyRNA are implemented in *[repository root]/source/blender/makesrna/intern/rna_internal_types.h*. StructRNA has a field named cont, of type ContainerRNA, shown in Listing 6-5.

Listing 6-5. The `ContainerRNA` data type implemented in [repository root]/source/blender/makesrna/intern/rna_internal_types.h. The next and prev fields point to `StructRNA` objects at the location of their "base" types, which are `ContainerRNA` objects. These are properties of an object's underlying "DNA" type

```
typedef struct ContainerRNA {
  void *next, *prev;

  struct GHash *prophash;
  ListBase properties;
} ContainerRNA;
```

BlenderRNA

The top-level "RNA" type called `BlenderRNA` (Listing 6-6) is instanced using `RNA_create()`. `RNA_create()` is prototyped in *RNA_define.h* (Listing 6-7). A `BlenderRNA` object wraps the "DNA" type called SDNA. SDNA was discussed in Chapter 2 and is defined in *[repository root]/source/blender/makesdna/DNA_sdna_types.h.*

Listing 6-6. The `BlenderRNA` implementation from [repository root]/source/blender/makesrna/intern/rna_internal_types.h

```
/* Blender RNA
 *
 * Root RNA data structure that lists all struct types. */

struct BlenderRNA {
  ListBase structs;
  /* A map of structs: {StructRNA.identifier -> StructRNA}
   * These are ensured to have unique names (with
     STRUCT_PUBLIC_NAMESPACE enabled). */
  struct GHash *structs_map;
```

```
/* Needed because types with an empty identifier aren't
   included in 'structs_map'. */
unsigned int structs_len;
};
```

Listing 6-7. RNA_create( ) from [repository root]/source/blender/
makesrna/intern/rna_define.c

```
BlenderRNA *RNA_create(void)
{
  BlenderRNA *brna;

  brna = MEM_callocN(sizeof(BlenderRNA), "BlenderRNA");
  const char *error_message = NULL;

  BLI_listbase_clear(&DefRNA.structs);
  brna->structs_map = BLI_ghash_str_new_ex(__func__, 2048);
...
  DefRNA.sdna = DNA_sdna_from_data(DNAstr, DNAlen, false,
  false, &error_message);
...
  return brna;
}
```

The "RNA" wrapper for the Main struct (blendfile data) is shown in
Listing 6-8. This definition is from the generated file *[build root]/source/
blender/makerna/intern/rna_main_gen.c.*

Listing 6-8. Definition of RNA_BlendData

```
StructRNA RNA_BlendData = {
    {(ContainerRNA *)&RNA_BlendDataCameras, (ContainerRNA
    *)&RNA_LineStyleTextureSlot,
    NULL,
```

```
  {(PropertyRNA *)&rna_BlendData_rna_properties,
  (PropertyRNA *)&rna_BlendData_lightprobes}},
  "BlendData", NULL, NULL, 516, NULL, "Blendfile Data",
  "Main data structure representing a .blend file and all
  its data-blocks",
  "*", 15,
  NULL, (PropertyRNA *)&rna_BlendData_rna_properties,
  NULL,
  NULL,
  NULL,
  NULL,
  NULL,
  NULL,
  NULL,
  NULL,
  {NULL, NULL}
};
```

PointerRNA

The definition of PointerRNA is shown in Listing 6-9 and Figure 6-3. In Listing 6-10, we see the implementation of RNA_main_pointer_create(). This function creates the PointerRNA used in the "RNA" Data API. Notice the RNA_BlendData variable, which is the definition for BlenderRNA. This RNA_* function adds the Main struct, which maintains Blender state.

Listing 6-9. PointerRNA type defined in [repository root]/source/ blender/makesrna/RNA_types.h. The data field is a pointer to the "DNA" struct that the "RNA" is wrapping

```
typedef struct PointerRNA {
  struct ID *owner_id;
```

```
    struct StructRNA *type;
    void *data;
} PointerRNA;
```

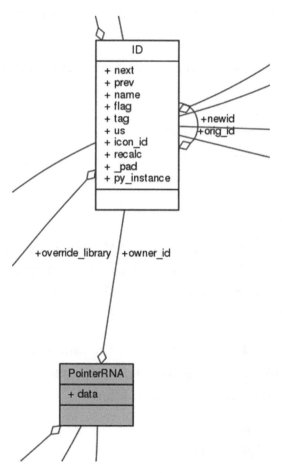

Figure 6-3. *Illustration of* `PointerRNA` *and its aggregation of* `ID`
struct

Listing 6-10. The PointerRNA defined for the Main struct ([repository root]/source/blender/makesrna/intern/rna_access.c). PointerRNA encapsulates "RNA" types used outside of the "RNA" API. RNA_BlendData is a variable defined by generated code in [build root]/source/blender/makesrna/intern/rna_main_gen.c

```
void RNA_main_pointer_create(struct Main *main, PointerRNA *r_ptr)
{
  r_ptr->owner_id = NULL;
  r_ptr->type = &RNA_BlendData;
  r_ptr->data = main;
}
```

PropertyRNA

PropertyRNA is the "base" type for all "RNA" property types. Listing 6-11 shows the PropertyRNA definition. Importantly, the mapping from "RNA" to "DNA" is done through an intermediary StructRNA, the type for the srna field in PropertyRNA.

Listing 6-11. The PropertyRNA struct definition from [repository root]/source/blender/makesrna/intern/rna_internal_types.h. The identifier and srna fields are in boldface

```
struct PropertyRNA {
  struct PropertyRNA *next, *prev;
  ...
  /* unique identifier */
  const char *identifier;
  ...

  /* This is used for accessing props/functions of this
     property
```

```
  * any property can have this but should only be used for
    collections and arrays
  * since python will convert int/bool/pointer's */
```

**struct StructRNA *srna; /* attributes attached directly to
this collection */**

```
/* python handle to hold all callbacks
  * (in a pointer array at the moment, may later be a tuple) */
void *py_data;
};
```

The backend Data API—not the interface—is part of the generated source. These functions populate a PropertyRNA object attached to the StructRNA, representing the corresponding "DNA" type. For instance, in Listing 6-12 we see struct BoolPropertyRNA. The function pointers get and set (of types PropBooleanGetFunc and PropBooleanSetFunc, respectively) are assigned accessors from generated code.

Listing 6-12. The struct BoolPropertyRNA definition from [repository root]/source/blender/makesrna/intern/rna_internal_types.h

```
typedef struct BoolPropertyRNA {
  PropertyRNA property;

  PropBooleanGetFunc get;
  PropBooleanSetFunc set;
  PropBooleanArrayGetFunc getarray;
  PropBooleanArraySetFunc setarray;

  PropBooleanGetFuncEx get_ex;
  PropBooleanSetFuncEx set_ex;
  PropBooleanArrayGetFuncEx getarray_ex;
  PropBooleanArraySetFuncEx setarray_ex;
```

```
    bool defaultvalue;
    const bool *defaultarray;
} BoolPropertyRNA;
```

In Listing 6-13, from *[repository root]/source/blender/makesrna/intern/ rna_light_gen.c,* we can see that rna_Light_type is represented with an "RNA" enumeration property. This translates to an EnumPropertyRNA field added to the corresponding StructRNA definition for that light type. rna_ Light_type is added to RNA_Light from Listing 6-4.

Listing 6-13. An EnumPropertyRNA object defined in [repository root]/source/blender/makesrna/intern/rna_light_gen.c. This is the rna_Light_type EnumPropertyRNA object shown as a property defined on RNA_Light (a StructRNA object)

```
EnumPropertyRNA rna_Light_type = {
    {(PropertyRNA *)&rna_Light_distance, NULL,
    -1, "type", 3, 0, 0, 0, 0, "Type",
    "Type of Light",
    0, "Light",
    PROP_ENUM, PROP_NONE | PROP_UNIT_NONE, NULL, 0, {0, 0,
    0}, 0,
    rna_Light_draw_update, 0, NULL, NULL, rna_property_
    override_diff_default, rna_property_override_store_
    default, rna_property_override_apply_default,
    0, -1, NULL},
    Light_type_get, Light_type_set, NULL, NULL, NULL, NULL,
    rna_Light_type_items, 4, 0
};
```

Generated "RNA" Code

As we have been alluding to, there is a substantial amount of code in makesrna that is generated. The generated code is written to the build directory and mirrors the *rna_*_.c* files from the *intern* subdirectory of the repository's makesrna module.

This code contains the appropriate "RNA" structs populated with values for extents, enumerations, and backend Data API functions. It is the RNA_* API that uses the functions in the generated code to directly interface "DNA."

The *makesrna.c* file is compiled to an executable and generates *rna_*_gen.c* files during the build process. Is there a list specifying each file and "DNA" type to be wrapped by the struct definitions from the generated source?

Turns out there is. Listing 6-14 shows PROCESS_ITEMS[], filled with RNAProcessItem objects. Each RNAProcessItem's define field is a function pointer to an RNA_def_* function, called by the *makesrna* executable to generate struct definitions for the "RNA" Data API. The RNA_def_* function is defined in a repository source file, in the filename field of the RNAProcessItem object.

Listing 6-14. RNAProcessItems and PROCESS_ITEMS[] from [repository root]/source/blender/makesrna/intern/makesrna.c. The RNAProcessItem for RNA_def_light is in boldface

```
typedef struct RNAProcessItem {
  const char *filename;
  const char *api_filename;
  void (*define)(BlenderRNA *brna);
} RNAProcessItem;

static RNAProcessItem PROCESS_ITEMS[] = {
    {"rna_rna.c", NULL, RNA_def_rna},
```

```
{"rna_ID.c", NULL, RNA_def_ID},
{"rna_texture.c", "rna_texture_api.c", RNA_def_texture},
...
```

{"rna_light.c", NULL, RNA_def_light},

```
...
```

Listing 6-15 shows code from *[repository root]/source/blender/
makesrna/intern/rna_light.c*. We can see the use of RNA_def_struct(),
RNA_def_struct_refine(), and RNA_def_struct_ui_text() for writing
out a definition of the StructRNA variable RNA_Light in *[build root]/source/
blender/makesrna/intern/rna_light_gen.c*. The *makesrna* executable calls
RNA_def_light() from its list of RNAProcessItem objects. The rna_def_*
functions are not runtime code. They are used only by the generation
phase during the build, to produce accessor and "RNA" properties'
runtime code for the Data API.

Listing 6-15. Example of RNA_define.h's API for creating "RNA"
from Light "DNA"

```
void RNA_def_light(BlenderRNA *brna)
{
  rna_def_light(brna);
  rna_def_point_light(brna);
  rna_def_area_light(brna);
  rna_def_spot_light(brna);
  rna_def_sun_light(brna);
}

static void rna_def_light(BlenderRNA *brna)
{
  StructRNA *srna;
  ...
  srna = RNA_def_struct(brna, "Light", "ID");
```

```
RNA_def_struct_sdna(srna, "Light");
RNA_def_struct_refine_func(srna, "rna_Light_refine");
RNA_def_struct_ui_text(srna, "Light", "Light
...
```

Setting Blender "DNA" Using "RNA"

The Data API provides a way for operators to update Blender "DNA." Operators use "RNA" properties to interface Blender "DNA." "RNA" properties map to "DNA" fields they abstract. This section's example is of an operator adding a point light object to a Blender scene. The example illustrates use of the Data API and its related "RNA" structs.

wmOperatorType

Blender operators are more than callback functions. We will cover them, in more detail, in Chapter 7. For now, they are represented by a wmOperatorType (Listing 6-16) and implemented in *[repository root]/source/blender/windowmanager/WM_types.h.*

Listing 6-16. The wmOperatorType implementation, showing relevant "RNA" related fields. The srna field is shown in boldface. srna points to a StructRNA

```
typedef struct wmOperatorType {
  /** Text for UI, undo. */
  const char *name;
  /** Unique identifier. */
  const char *idname;
...
  /** rna for properties */
  struct StructRNA *srna;
```

```
...
  /**
   * Default rna property to use for generic invoke functions.
   * menus, enum search... etc. Example: Enum 'type' for a
     Delete menu.
   *
   * When assigned a string/number property,
   * immediately edit the value when used in a popup. see:
     #UI_BUT_ACTIVATE_ON_INIT.
   */
  PropertyRNA *prop;
...

  /** RNA integration */
  ExtensionRNA ext;
...
} wmOperatorType;
```

The wmOperatorType struct contains groups of related "RNA" properties derived from the underlying "DNA" type it acts upon. The operator may either "get" or "set" these individual properties via the Data API.

Adding a Light

We just covered the preliminaries. We now discuss the data structures and function calls for extracting settings information in an operator using the Data API and "RNA."

The Blender Python API function bpy.ops.object.light_add() creates a new light object. It is an operator invoked using bpy.ops (the operators submodule of bpy).

Note   Operators are implemented in C code, but it is possible to write operators in Python as well. Python-based operators are run by the Blender Python extended interpreter. In this chapter, however, we show the Blender Python API calling a C based operator.

A call stack for this operator's execution is shown in Figure 6-4.

```
≡ BKE_light_add() at light.c:62 0x55555778f7f6
≡ BKE_object_obdata_add_from_type() at object.c:854
≡ object_add_common() at object.c:923 0x5555577f68b
≡ BKE_object_add() at object.c:945 0x5555577f691f
≡ ED_object_add_type() at object_add.c:489 0x55555582
≡ object_light_add_exec() at object_add.c:1,259 0x5555
≡ wm_operator_invoke() at wm_event_system.c:1,279 0
≡ wm_operator_call_internal() at wm_event_system.c:1,
≡ WM_operator_call_py() at wm_event_system.c:1,614 0
≡ pyop_call() at bpy_operator.c:268 0x555558080d56
```

Figure 6-4. *Call stack starting from* `pyop_call()` *in [repository root]/source/blender/python/intern/bpy_operator.c*

Relevant "RNA"

In this example, the operator's action simply creates a new point light. The pertinent attributes ("properties") are ones associated with a point light. Only a subset of attributes are relevant in the "DNA" Light, for example, its area_shape field is not used.

In this case, these properties are those of the global variable RNA_ PointLight, a StructRNA. RNA_PointLight is defined in the "RNA" generated code. Its definition is shown in Listing 6-17.

Listing 6-17. The RNA_PointLight global variable defined in [build root]/source/blender/makesrna/intern/rna_light_gen.c. The cont field (ContainerRNA type) assignment is shown in boldface, along with the FloatPropertyRNA type rna_PointLight_energy, just one of the multiple "RNA" properties

```
StructRNA RNA_PointLight = {
    {(ContainerRNA *)&RNA_AreaLight, (ContainerRNA *)&RNA_
    Light,
    NULL,
    {(PropertyRNA *)&rna_PointLight_energy, (PropertyRNA
    *)&rna_PointLight_contact_shadow_thickness}},
    "PointLight", NULL, NULL, 519, NULL, "Point Light",
    "Omnidirectional point Light",
    "*", 298,
    (PropertyRNA *)&rna_ID_name, (PropertyRNA *)&rna_ID_rna_
    properties,
    &RNA_Light,
    NULL,
    rna_Light_refine,
    NULL,
    NULL,
    NULL,
    rna_ID_instance,
    rna_ID_idprops,
    {NULL, NULL}
};
```

Relevant "RNA" properties are stored by wmOperatorType's srna field, a pointer to a StructRNA. Note that each of the "DNA" types has a set of global StructRNA variables defined in the "RNA" generated code. For the "DNA" type instance, Light from *[repository root]/source/blender/*

makesdna/DNA_light_types.h has its StructRNA definitions in *[build root]/ source/blender/makesrna/intern/rna_light_gen.c.* We just saw an example of this with RNA_PointLight. A StructRNA's "RNA" properties are each represented by a PropertyRNA object. There is a "derived" PropertyRNA type for each "RNA" property: BoolPropertyRNA, IntPropertyRNA, etc.

Note   Recall that there is no language mechanism in C that explicitly enables inheritance. It is approximated by including the base type as a header in the "derived" struct. We saw this with PyObject in Chapter 5.

---

rna_PointLight_energy, a FloatPropertyRNA, is shown in Listing 6-18. It illustrates "getter" and "setter" functions for that property.

Listing 6-18. The rna_PointLight_energy "RNA" property, from [build root]/source/blender/makesrna/intern/rna_light_gen.c. The associated "getter" and "setter" for this property are also shown. These accessor functions directly manipulate the Light "DNA" struct

```
/* Point Light */
FloatPropertyRNA rna_PointLight_energy = {
    {(PropertyRNA *)&rna_PointLight_falloff_type, NULL,
    -1, "energy", 3, 0, 0, 4, 0, "Power",
    "Amount of light emitted",
    0, "*",
    PROP_FLOAT, PROP_POWER | PROP_UNIT_POWER, NULL, 0, {0, 0,
    0}, 0,
    rna_Light_draw_update, 0, NULL, NULL, rna_property_
    override_diff_default, rna_property_override_store_
    default, rna_property_override_apply_default,
```

```
        offsetof(Light, energy), 5, NULL},
    PointLight_energy_get, PointLight_energy_set, NULL, NULL,
    NULL, NULL, NULL, NULL, NULL, NULL, 0.0f, 1000000.0f,
    -FLT_MAX, FLT_MAX, 10.0f, 5, 10.0f, NULL
};

float PointLight_energy_get(PointerRNA *ptr)
{
    Light *data = (Light *)(ptr->data);
    return (float)(data->energy);
}

void PointLight_energy_set(PointerRNA *ptr, float value)
{
    Light *data = (Light *)(ptr->data);
    data->energy = value;
}
```

The light object "types" are all eventually represented by the general
Light struct (a "DNA" type). Each, however, is represented only by a
subset of Light's fields. Thus, the related properties for each light "type"
(e.g., point, area, etc.) are chained together in the cont field of StructRNA,
for access during an operator's action.

The container of properties will be used to set the correct variables in
Light. Recalling Listing 6-17, notice the container of properties in RNA_
PointLight's cont field.

Calling the Data API

Starting at pyop_call() in Listing 6-19, a PointerRNA object is created to
wrap the operator's properties. A PointerRNA contains a StructRNA object.

Listing 6-19. Start of the operator in pyop_call() from [repository root]/source/blender/python/intern/bpy_operator.c. A PointerRNA is created

```
static PyObject *pyop_call(PyObject *UNUSED(self), PyObject
*args)
{
  wmOperatorType *ot;
  int error_val = 0;
  PointerRNA ptr;
...
  ot = WM_operatortype_find(opname, true);
...
    WM_operator_properties_create_ptr(&ptr, ot);
    WM_operator_properties_sanitize(&ptr, 0);
...
        operator_ret = WM_operator_call_py(C, ot, context,
        &ptr, reports, is_undo);
...
```

We see that a PointerRNA object is defined in a call to WM_operator_ properties_create_ptr(), using the correct operator type ot, retrieved from WM_operatortype_find().

WM_operator_call_py() is passed the ptr variable with the appropriate StructRNA properties for the operator type obtained earlier by WM_operatortype_find().

The execution path eventually reaches wm_operator_invoke() after a few prior calls seen in Figure 6-4. The PointerRNA is passed to each of these calls, eventually landing in wm_operator_invoke(). It is here that a wmOperator (Listing 6-20) is created.

Listing 6-20. `wm_operator_invoke()` from [repository root]/source/blender/windowmanager/intern/wm_event_system.c

```
static int wm_operator_invoke(bContext *C,
                              wmOperatorType *ot,
                              wmEvent *event,
                              PointerRNA *properties,
                              ReportList *reports,
                              const bool poll_only,
                              bool use_last_properties)
{
...
    wmOperator *op = wm_operator_create(wm, ot, properties,
    reports);
...
        retval = op->type->exec(C, op);
...
```

The `wmOperator` returned from `wm_operator_create()` houses a `PointerRNA`. The `PointerRNA` itself contains the proper `StructRNA` with our "RNA" properties for the operator. `struct wmOperator` is shown in Listing 6-21.

Listing 6-21. Elided `struct wmOperator` defined in [repository root]/source/blender/makesdna/DNA_windowmanager_types.h

```
typedef struct wmOperator {
...
  /** Rna pointer to access properties. */
  struct PointerRNA *ptr;
...
} wmOperator;
```

We now reach object_light_add_exec(), shown in Figure 6-4. object_light_add_exec() is the first function in the operator execution path that uses the Data API. Here, a "DNA" type Light is pointed to by the variable la. See Listing 6-22.

Listing 6-22. Snippet from the object_light_add_exec() definition, in [repository root]/source/blender/editors/object/object_add.c

```
static int object_light_add_exec(bContext *C, wmOperator *op)
{
  Object *ob;
  Light *la;
...
  float loc[3], rot[3];
... ED_object_add_generic_get_opts(C, op, 'Z', loc, rot, NULL,
&local_view_bits, NULL))
...
  ob = ED_object_add_type(C, OB_LAMP, get_light_defname(type),
  loc, rot, false, local_view_bits);
...
  return OPERATOR_FINISHED;
}
```

In object_light_add_exec(), we make a call to ED_object_add_generic_get_opts(), using the Data API to extract options such as the intended location for the light.

Listing 6-23. ED_object_add_generic_get_opts() obtains settings required by wmOperator, using the Data API. Here, we see the Data API call RNA_float_get_array() for the location variable loc. The loc variable is gathered from the PointerRNA data field, which points to an ID (struct header) contained in the Object struct (not shown) of the Light "DNA" object

```
bool ED_object_add_generic_get_opts(bContext *C,
                           wmOperator *op,
                           const char view_align_axis,
                           float loc[3],
                           float rot[3],
                           bool *enter_editmode,
                           ushort *local_view_bits,
                           bool *is_view_aligned)
{
...
   /* Location! */
   {
     float _loc[3];
     if (!loc) {
       loc = _loc;
     }

     if (RNA_struct_property_is_set(op->ptr, "location")) {
       RNA_float_get_array(op->ptr, "location", loc);
     }
...
```

"DNA" via the **blenkernel** Module

For completion of an operator's action, we look at ED_object_add_type(). This function is called by object_light_add_exec() and uses the BKE_* API. We do not trace the code to BKE_light_add(). However, this operator eventually inserts the new light into the appropriate "collection" (a linked list of objects using ListBase as the field type) in the Main struct.

ED_object_add_type() passes settings garnered by the Data API and passes them to the blenkernel API. See Listing 6-24.

Note   Up to this point in the call stack, we have wended through different modules. We can see the editors module plays a key role in operator actions. We will look more at the editors module in Chapter 7 and 8.

Listing 6-24. ED_object_add_type() from [repository root]/source/ blender/editors/object/object_add.c. We now have the proper settings from the "RNA" and can use the copied data to write to "DNA." Notice the CTX_* API from the blenkernel module, to get bmain, scene, and view_layer from the bContext parameter

```
Object *ED_object_add_type(bContext *C,
                           int type,
                           const char *name,
                           const float loc[3],
                           const float rot[3],
                           bool enter_editmode,
                           ushort local_view_bits)
{
  Main *bmain = CTX_data_main(C);
  Scene *scene = CTX_data_scene(C);
  ViewLayer *view_layer = CTX_data_view_layer(C);
  Object *ob;
...
    ob = BKE_object_add(bmain, scene, view_layer, type, name);
...
  return ob;
}
```

The **python** Module and Blender "RNA"

We just saw an example of a Blender Python API operator call. But how does the Blender Python API connect to the "RNA" Data API in the first place?

We already know how the Blender Python API extensions are created in the python module from Chapter 5. There, we had shown that each extension module is represented by a PyObject "derived" type, using PyTypeObject from the CPython library to define the classes and methods (or functions) that compose a Blender Python API module.

Now, we need to investigate the specific PyObject plus PyTypeObject derivatives with connections to Blender "RNA." We will do this for the bpy. data Python API submodule, which provides access to the Main struct of the Blender "DNA." (The mechanism for doing this is similar for other Blender Python API connections to Blender "RNA," such as the bpy. ops.object.light_add() call.) For access to the Main "DNA" struct, we need pyrna_struct_getattro() and pyrna_struct_setattro()—their function definitions provided in *[repository root]/source/blender/python/ intern/bpy_rna.c*.

Both are invoked by pyop_call(). The path to their execution is similar to the call stack in Figure 6-4. However, these functions need to be connected to the respective PyObject. How does this happen?

The particular PyObject we are interested in is called BPy_StructRNA. It is shown in Listing 6-25 and the collaboration diagram in Figure 6-5.

Listing 6-25. struct BPy_StructRNA from [repository root]/source/ blender/python/intern/bpy_rna.h. The struct is elided to reveal the PointerRNA field, shown in boldface. We know struct BPy_ StructRNA is a PyObject because it contains a PyObject_HEAD

```
typedef struct {
  PyObject_HEAD /* required python macro   */
```

...

PointerRNA ptr;

...

} BPy_StructRNA;

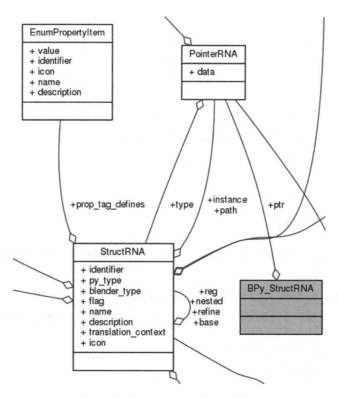

Figure 6-5. *The* BPy_StructRNA *collaboration diagram*

We see that BPy_StructRNA really serves to hold the PointerRNA object, which encapsulates the underlying StructRNA. The StructRNA allows the execution path to lead to the backend Data API functions that access the Blender "DNA." As shown previously in this chapter, we need to point the data field of PointerRNA, to its "DNA" object.

Listing 6-26 shows the process for the Main struct. This is a python module API function that returns a struct BPy_StructRNA object (a PyObject "derived" type).

Listing 6-26. Wrapping the Main struct with a PointerRNA object and then creating the corresponding struct BPy_StructRNA to register as a PyObject. This will provide access to the embedded Python interpreter. This is performed by BPY_rna_module(), from [repository root]/source/blender/python/intern/bpy_rna.c

```
/* 'bpy.data' from Python. */
static PointerRNA *rna_module_ptr = NULL;
PyObject *BPY_rna_module(void)
{
  BPy_StructRNA *pyrna;
  PointerRNA ptr;

  /* For now, return the base RNA type rather than a real
  module. */
  RNA_main_pointer_create(G_MAIN, &ptr);
  pyrna = (BPy_StructRNA*)pyrna_struct_CreatePyObject(&ptr);

  rna_module_ptr = &pyrna->ptr;
  return (PyObject *)pyrna;
}
```

In Listing 6-27, we see the pyrna_struct_getattro() and pyrna_struct_setattro() functions and where they are added to the PyTypeObject derived type. Recall that the PyTypeObject fields are numerous and its methods are added as arrays of PyGetSetDef, depending on the nature of the methods or functions being added.

Listing 6-27. The struct BPy_StructRNA functions for access to the Main struct "DNA" are defined in [repository root]/source/blender/python/intern/bpy_rna.c. The tp_getattro and tp_setattro function pointer fields of PyTypeObject are used for pyrna_struct_getattro() and pyrna_struct_setattro(), respectively

```
PyTypeObject pyrna_struct_Type = {
    PyVarObject_HEAD_INIT(NULL, 0) "bpy_struct", /* tp_name */
    sizeof(BPy_StructRNA),                       /* tp_basicsize */
    ...
    (getattrofunc)pyrna_struct_getattro, /* getattrofunc tp_
    getattro; */
    (setattrofunc)pyrna_struct_setattro, /* setattrofunc tp_
    setattro; */
    ...
    NULL,
};
```

Summary

This chapter covered "RNA" and the Data API. We have seen that the makerna module is different from other Blender modules. The purpose of makesrna is to implement wrappers for "DNA" types, so that operators can interface "DNA" using value ranges, accessor functions, etc.

Much of the code is generated from function calls using the makesrna API, that is, functions with the prefix RNA_def_*. The other makesrna API functions form the "RNA" Data API interface. They are prototyped in the *RNA_access.h* file.

Generated and repository source files, together, provide the backend for the Data API. This code performs the data manipulations on "DNA" structs.

Finally, we saw how the Blender Python API, as implemented in the python module, connects the PyObjects which represent the extended Blender CPython to the "RNA" interface of the Data API.

## CHAPTER 7

The **editors** Module, Operators, and Event System

We have covered aspects of supporting code (e.g., GHOST, blenlib, python, etc.), which allows for higher-level functionality—that of the windowmanager module, and in this chapter the editors module. Even when discussing support code, it is impossible to delineate these modules as entirely autonomous subsystems. We have tried to approximate this, at times avoiding dependencies and some Blender codebase paradigms. Now, in this chapter, we cover the editors module. More specifically, we discuss how the editors module registers and implements Blender's editors. We then describe in more detail operators themselves and their composition. We will cover the connections between editors and the windowmanager module—as it is responsible for initializing operators and editors—as well as being the hub for events.

Editors

The editors module, put succinctly, contains the code that defines the different views and operations on Blender data. Blender's graphical user interface (GUI) has a number of editor categories, for example, "General,"

B. E. Hollister, *Core Blender Development*,
https://doi.org/10.1007/978-1-4842-6415-7_7

"Animation," "Scripting," and "Data." A few editors are "3D Viewport," "Image Editor," "Text Editor," "Outliner," etc. Each editor provides a separate view, where each visualizes different parts of the Blender data or "DNA." Editors also usually allow for changing (e.g., editing, deleting, or adding to) "DNA," where upon their view is updated accordingly.

We already know operators (i.e., their callbacks) are ultimately responsible for updating "DNA." We start our exploration, therefore, by explaining the "core" data types associated with editors, not all of which are implemented within the editors module. For instance, editors are part of the Blender state and as such can be saved to file. Therefore, some of their struct's are thus "DNA" and implemented in the makesdna module.

The editors module provides both its ED_* API and also the UI_* API. The UI_* API provides services for GUI layout and widgets, all native to the Blender codebase. We will discuss the UI_* API in the next chapter, when our focus is GUI elements.

Directory Layout and Files

Unlike other Blender modules with their headers (API function prototypes) and an *intern* subdirectory, the editors module is flattened into a set of only subdirectories. These directories hold operator-only code grouped by the data they act upon, the editor API, user-interface API, or the "space types" code, which is often a mixture of editor definitions and editor-specific operators. We see the editors module directory contents in Figure 7-1.

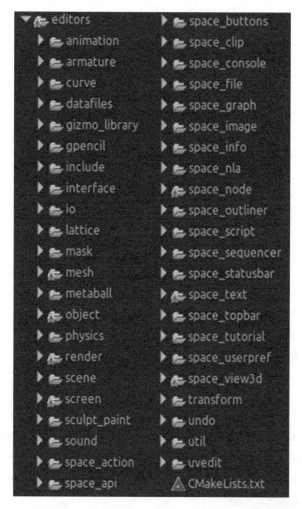

Figure 7-1. *The* editors *module contents located at source/blender/ editors/. The editor definitions (including operators acting only from the given editor) are located in the directories prefaced with* space_*. *Other directories hold operator registration and callback implementations for operators grouped by the Blender data they affect. Notice the* space_tutorial *folder. This will be covered later in the next chapter, and is not part of the original Blender repository*

As an example, the "outliner" editor visualizes the active scene. In Figure 7-2, the *space_outliner* subdirectory files are listed.

Figure 7-2. *The "outliner" editor's source files. These are located at source/blender/editors/space_outliner/*

The *space_outliner.c* file contains the registration function, called from the windowmanager module. The callbacks (not the creation and initialization functions) are defined in the other files. This is the usual pattern for the other editors, unless the editor's implementation is relatively short and entirely within a single *space_*.c* file, for example, the contents of *space_topbar*.

The ED_* API implementation is stored in the *space_api* subdirectory, and the ED_* prototypes are in the sibling subdirectory *include*. The entire ED_* API is implemented in the source file *spacetypes.c*. In addition to the ED_* prototypes, /include/ also contains the UI_* API prototypes and a file called *BIF_glutil.h* (abbreviation for "Blender Image Functions OpenGL Utilities"). *BIF_glutil.h* provides ED_* prototypes related to drawing images, primarily for icon images and other user interface rendering. The UI_* API function definitions are in *interface*.

Editor **Structs**: The "Space" Types

Data and "member" functions for Blender editor definitions are kept in various structs. These records are of the SpaceType struct, and derivatives of the SpaceLink struct (Listing 7-1). The construction of editor objects is similar to PyObjects from the CPython API, discussed earlier in this book. SpaceLink is analogous to PyObject, and SpaceType is analogous to PyTypeObject.

You will recall that PyObject is a "base" type and is required at the beginning of every struct-type implementation that derives from it. The CPython API provides a macro (PyObject_HEAD) to facilitate this. However, structs that derive from SpaceLink do not use a macro, and such types simply reimplement the SpaceLink fields. There is even a comment prior to the SpaceLink definition that apparently suggests this discrepancy.

Listing 7-1. SpaceLink struct from source/blender/makesdna/ DNA_space_types.h. The SpaceLink struct is the "base" type for "concrete" editor types. Each SpaceLink allows "linking" into the linkedlist of all other editors in Main, using its next and prev fields. This is a convention in the Blender codebase. Note the comment included from the source file

```
/**
 * The base structure all the other spaces
 * are derived (implicitly) from. Would be
 * good to make this explicit.
 */
typedef struct SpaceLink {
  struct SpaceLink *next, *prev;
  /** Storage of regions for inactive spaces. */
  ListBase regionbase;
  char spacetype;
```

```
    char link_flag;
    char _pad0[6];
} SpaceLink;
```

Looking at the SpaceLink variables, you can see a field named spacetype. The spacetype field stores a numerical code from 0 to 255, representing the type of editor. These values are defined as an enum, called eSpace_Type, defined in *source/blender/makesdna/DNA_space_types.h*.

As you will recall, the "DNA" types are serialized, so throughout you will see _pad* fields for byte-alignment in "DNA" structs, discussed in Chapter 2. The SpaceLink reimplementation, at the head of the SpaceFile definition, is shown in boldface in Listing 7-2.

Listing 7-2. SpaceFile is an example "derived" type from SpaceLink. It is implemented in source/blender/makesdna/DNA_space_types.h. Each of the editors has its own derived type from SpaceLink

```
/* File Browser */
typedef struct SpaceFile {
  SpaceLink *next, *prev;
  /** Storage of regions for inactive spaces. */
  ListBase regionbase;
  char spacetype;
  char link_flag;
  char _pad0[6];
  /* End 'SpaceLink' header. */

  char _pad1[4];
  int scroll_offset;
  ...

} SpaceFile;
```

As "member" functions are not editor data, they are stored separately in the SpaceType struct. As a consequence, the SpaceType struct implementation is contained in *source/blender/blenkernel/BKE_screen.h* outside of the makesdna module, as SpaceType is not Blender "DNA." Another slight discrepancy is that SpaceType.spaceid is of type int, while SpaceLink.spacetype is of type char. These two fields are assigned the identical enum (e.g., SPACE_OUTLINER), for the SpaceLink and SpaceType object pair representing any particular editor. A code snippet of the SpaceType struct is shown in Listing 7-3.

Listing 7-3. An elided SpaceType listing from source/blender/ blenkernel/BKE_screen.h. The new and free function pointer fields are shown in boldface, whereas the remaining "member" functions are not for brevity. You also will notice that there is a list of regiontypes. We will discuss regions in the next section

```
typedef struct SpaceType {
  struct SpaceType *next, *prev;

  char name[BKE_ST_MAXNAME]; /* for menus */
  int spaceid;                    /* unique space identifier */
  int iconid;                     /* icon lookup for menus */

  /* Initial allocation, after this WM will call init() too.
     Some editors need
   * area and scene data (e.g. frame range) to set their
     initial scrolling. */
  struct SpaceLink *(*new)(const struct ScrArea *sa, const
  struct Scene *scene);
  /* not free spacelink itself */
  void (*free)(struct SpaceLink *sl);

  ...
```

```
/* region type definitions */
ListBase regiontypes;
...

} SpaceType;
```

Editor Registration

Editors are registered in WM_init(), by a call to ED_spacetype_init(). This function is shown in Listing 7-4. Each function for creating space types is provided by the individual editor. This process amounts to providing function pointers for initialization, etc.

Also, in any given ED_spacetype_*() listed in ED_spacetype_init(), the "region" types (ARegionType struct) are added to the lists of "region" types associated with the SpaceType struct object, for the editor. We will see a specific example of this in the next chapter, where we write our own custom editor.

At the end of ED_spacetype_init(), all of the editors' SpaceType. operatortype function pointers are called to register operator types. We will discuss operator registration later in this chapter.

Listing 7-4. ED_spacetypes_init() in source/blender/editors/ space_api/spacetypes.c. Gizmos are beyond the scope of this book

```
/* only call once on startup, storage is global in BKE kernel
listbase */
void ED_spacetypes_init(void)
{
  const ListBase *spacetypes;
  SpaceType *type;
  ...
  /* create space types */
  ED_spacetype_outliner();
```

```
ED_spacetype_view3d();
ED_spacetype_ipo();
...

spacetypes = BKE_spacetypes_list();
for (type = spacetypes->first; type; type = type->next) {
  ...
  if (type->operatortypes) {
    type->operatortypes();
  }
}
}
```

Each ED_spactype_*() call adds its SpaceType object to the global
spactypes ListBase (as seen in Listing 7-5) via BKE_spacetype_
register().

Listing 7-5. The global spacetypes ListBase stores each
SpaceType object in source/blender/blenkernel/intern/screen.c.
This list is appended whenever an editor is registered

```
/* keep global; this has to be accessible outside of
windowmanager */
static ListBase spacetypes = {NULL, NULL};
```

In the init field of the SpaceType ("area") or ARegionType ("regions"),
the function provided there will add handlers. We cover ScrArea and
ARegion structs and their use later in the chapter. These handlers are
objects of the wmEventHandler struct shown in Listing 7-6.

There is a poll function of type EventHandlerPoll that takes ARegion
and wmEvent parameter types (function type definition not shown). This
struct type is a "base" type for derived types. The wmKeyMap struct (also
defined in *wm_event_system.h*) is "derived" and provides a set of key codes
(enums) that should be handled for the "area" or "region."

Listing 7-6. The wmEventHandler struct is added to ScrArea and ARegion objects, to denote which types of events are handled. This struct is implemented in source/blender/windowmanager/ wm_event_system.h.

```
typedef struct wmEventHandler {
  struct wmEventHandler *next, *prev;

  enum eWM_EventHandlerType type;
  char flag; /* WM_HANDLER_BLOCKING, ... */

  EventHandlerPoll poll;
} wmEventHandler;
```

windowmanager Revisit: Windows, "Screens," "Areas," and "Regions"

There is a tight coupling between the windowmanager and editors modules. All editors must live in a "space" (sometimes called a "Screen Area," or more simply "area") within a Blender application window. Thus, we will cover the object (record) hierarchies that maintain state, and that point to handlers, for the various grouping levels of a window's real estate. These constructs are definitions of the Blender codebase, and not offered by the underlying operating system's window API.

At the highest level, all Blender windows are managed by the windowmanager module, as its title implies. We saw that the windowmanager module is a wrapper for GHOST, which is itself a wrapper for the underlying operating system's windowing API. Of course, each wrapper assumes various application-specific qualities. This becomes apparent in Blender, at the windowmanager module level. As such, Blender maintains a list of its window objects in the wmWindowManager struct, seen in UML in Figure 7-3.

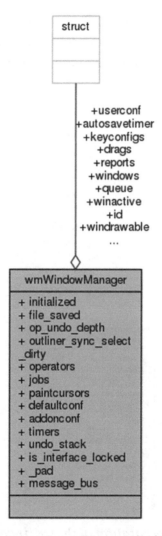

Figure 7-3. *UML representation of the* `wmWindowManager` `struct`
*defined in source/blender/makesdna/DNA_windowmanager_*
types.h. We see the field `windows`, *which is an aggregation of* `struct-`
type objects pointed to from `wmWindowManager`

Blender application windows are represented by the `wmWindow`
struct-type. A UML representation can be seen in Figure 7-4. Here,
the `wmWindow` struct points back to its GHOST window, which it builds

from. Below the wmWindow level, the Blender user interface divides the application window into editors. Editors have already been described semantically, that is, in terms of their purpose in the Blender application.

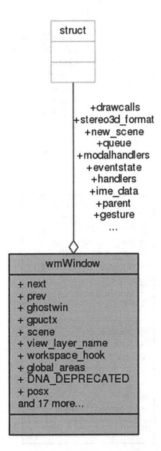

Figure 7-4. *UML representation of the* wmWindow struct *defined in source/blender/makesdna/DNA_windowmanager_types.h.* wmWindow *represents a Blender window object. It has a pointer to a GHOST window (its* void *ghostwin *field), the underlying application window created by GHOST from the host operating system*

We have also looked at their implementation somewhat, regarding the structs that represent editor state and point to "member" functions that need to be defined in the particular space_* subdirectory, in the editors module.

However, the mechanics of the user interface divides a Blender application window into a top-level "screen" (the part of an application's window that is the OpenGL context render surface). The bScreen struct is shown in Listing 7-7.

Listing 7-7. The bScreen struct from source/blender/makesdna/ DNA_screen_types.h. The two-dimensional geometry of the screen is stored in window (pixel) coordinates using the ScrVert and ScrEdge struct types. The screen vertices and edges delineate each screen area, stored as ScrArea objects. While the bScreen maintains the deprecated fields, these attributes are now contained in a ScrAreaMap struct. The ScrAreaMap fields of the bScreen struct are shown in boldface

```
typedef struct bScreen {
  ID id;
  ...
  /** Screens have vertices/edges to define areas. */
  ListBase vertbase;
  ListBase edgebase;
  ListBase areabase;

  /** Screen level regions (menus), runtime only. */
  ListBase regionbase;
  ...
} bScreen;
```

This "screen" is further divided into "areas," which represent editors. The ScrArea struct implementation is shown in the snippet from

Listing 7-8. The ScrVert pointers v1, v2, v3, and v4 in ScrArea point to the vertbase vertices from the ScrAreaMap struct, contained in bScreen.

Listing 7-8. An elided ScrArea struct implementation from source/blender/makesdna/DNA_screen_types.h. We see here in boldface the fields that point to the associated SpaceType and SpaceLink structs defining an editor represented by the ScrArea object. Below these fields, we also can see further down the editor hierarchy with the regionbase field. Also, the handlers field is shown which is the list of objects that connect to functions for events handled by "area" level-of-concern in an editor (more on this later)

```
typedef struct ScrArea {
  struct ScrArea *next, *prev;

  /** Ordered (bl, tl, tr, br). */
  ScrVert *v1, *v2, *v3, *v4;
  /** If area==full, this is the parent. */
  bScreen *full;

  /** Rect bound by v1 v2 v3 v4. */
  rcti totrct;
  ...
  char spacetype;
  ...
  struct SpaceType *type;
  ...
  /** #SpaceLink. */
  ListBase spacedata;
  ...
  /** #ARegion. */
  ListBase regionbase;
  /** #wmEventHandler. */
```

```
ListBase handlers;
  ...
} ScrArea;
```

Further still, an "area" is divided into "regions." One or more "regions" compose an editor's "area." There are two types that represent "regions" in the Blender codebase: ARegion and ARegionType (shown in Listings 7-9 and 7-10, respectively). The ARegion and ARegionType structs follow the same convention for data and "member" function encapsulation, as did the SpaceLink and SpaceType structs for top-level editor concerns.

Listing 7-9. Partial ARegion struct from source/blender/makesdna/DNA_screen_types.h. Here, we have list pointers for the multiple "regions" in an "area." Also, there are fields related to the geometry and two-dimensional drawing of an ARegion object. We will talk more about View2D, etc. in the next chapter on user interface code and 2D drawing, in the Blender codebase

```
typedef struct ARegion {
  struct ARegion *next, *prev;

  /** 2D-View scrolling/zoom info (most regions are 2d
      anyways). */
  View2D v2d;
  /** Coordinates of region. */
  rcti winrct;
  /** Runtime for partial redraw, same or smaller than winrct. */
  rcti drawrct;
  /** Size. */
  short winx, winy;
  ...
} ARegion;
```

Listing 7-10. A partial `ARegionType` `struct` listing from source/ blender/blenkernel/BKE_screen.h. The ARegionType contains handler functions for "region" level concerns in the editor. These are primarily of the user interface drawing and updating variety and will be looked at more closely in the next chapter

```
typedef struct ARegionType {
  struct ARegionType *next, *prev;

  int regionid; /* unique identifier within this space, defines
  RGN_TYPE_xxxx */

  /* add handlers, stuff you only do once or on area/region
     type/size changes */
  void (*init)(struct wmWindowManager *wm, struct ARegion *ar);
  ...
} ARegionType;
```

Below the level of "region" are panels and active zones. We will not cover active zones, but panels will be discussed more in the next chapter on the Blender UI API.

The source code has an explanation of this, partially shown in Listing 7-11. In the listing, you can see a window's screen divisions and the struct names associated with each division, that is, `ScrArea` and `ARegion`. This particular example assumes the standard modeling layout and would differ if another layout was selected or configured by the user.

Listing 7-11. Part of the Blender window layout explanation from source/blender/windowmanager/WM_types.h. Here, we see a hypothetical `wmWindow`'s `bScreen`, with its "area" and "region" divisions

```
+---------------------------------------------------------------+
|+---------------------------------------------+-------------+ |
||ScrArea (links to 3D view)                    |ScrArea      | |
||+-------++----------+-------------------+|(links to      | |
|||ARegion||          |ARegion (quad view)|| properties) | |
||||(tools)||          |                   ||             | |
|||       ||          |                   ||             | |
|||       ||          |                   ||             | |
|||       ||          |                   ||             | |
|||       |+----------+-------------------+|             | |
|||       ||          |                   ||             | |
|||       ||          |                   ||             | |
|||       ||          |                   ||             | |
|||       ||          |                   ||             | |
|||       ||          |                   ||             | |
||+-------++----------+-------------------+|             | |
|+---------------------------------------------+-------------+ |
+---------------------------------------------------------------+
```

Blender's Operators

In the last chapter, we saw an example of using "RNA" to store property data in operators. At that time, however, we did not talk specifically about how operators are registered, or the particular callbacks that they may contain.

This section discusses the following about the implementation of the Blender operators:

- The data types wmOperatorType and wmOperator

- Operator registration

- Required callbacks for operators

- How operators connect as handlers to editors

- The handling of events using operators

The Operator **Structs**: **wmOperatorType** and **wmOperator**

Operators are defined by two structs in Blender:

- wmOperatorType

- wmOperator

WM_init() is called at the start of the Blender application. There two functions, wm_operator_type_init() and wm_operatortypes_register(), are invoked. The purpose of these two functions is to create objects of the wmOperatorType struct, by setting these objects' fields for a given operation registration. The wmOperatorType struct is shown in Listing 7-12.

Listing 7-12. Elided wmOperatorType struct implementation from source/blender/windowmanager/WM_types.h. Only two callback function pointer fields are shown: exec and poll. The exec field provides a function to perform the action of a "non-modal" operator, while the poll field provides a function to check the context of the operator call, via an event such as a Python script execution or keypress event

```
typedef struct wmOperatorType {
```

```
/** Text for UI, undo. */
const char *name;
/** Unique identifier. */
const char *idname;
...
int (*exec)(struct bContext *, struct wmOperator *) ATTR_
WARN_UNUSED_RESULT;
...
bool (*poll)(struct bContext *) ATTR_WARN_UNUSED_RESULT;
...
/** rna for properties */
struct StructRNA *srna;
...
/** pointer to modal keymap, do not free! */
struct wmKeyMap *modalkeymap;
...
} wmOperatorType;
```

Not all of the functions for a particular operator need to be provided. The wmOperatorType actually allows for ten possible callbacks. In total, these are

- exec
- check
- invoke
- cancel
- modal
- poll
- poll_property
- ui

- get_name

- get_description

Some of the other functions provide the ability to perform modal operations, such as invoke, modal, and check, etc. Modal operators are like modal windows (or dialogs). Their callbacks are repeatedly called during the operator process, until the user finishes the operation. Non-modal operators do not require these callbacks to be defined.

Before we continue with our discussion of callbacks, let us first discuss the wmOperator struct. The wmOperator struct is shown in Listing 7-13. wmOperator is implemented in the makesdna module, thus making it Blender "DNA" and serializable.

Listing 7-13. Partial snippet of wmOperator from source/blender/makesdna/DNA_windowmanager_types.h

```
typedef struct wmOperator {
  struct wmOperator *next, *prev;
  /* saved */
  /** Used to retrieve type pointer. */
  char idname[64];
  ...
  /* runtime */
  /** Operator type definition from idname. */
  struct wmOperatorType *type;
  ...
  /** Rna pointer to access properties. */
  struct PointerRNA *ptr;
  ...
} wmOperator;
```

Take notice of the following fields:

- The wmOperator pointers next and prev

- The char array (string) idname

- The pointer to a wmOperatorType type

- The PointerRNA pointer ptr

There are more fields, some of which are responsible for storing data during an operator's processing and others related to the Python API.

The wmOperator struct works as a record, in order for Blender's code to handle events by allowing access to the necessary functions and data. Note that the wmOperator struct type is defined in makesdna, making it persistent. This allows for the operator stack to be saved to the blend file as well.

There are many more types defined in *source/blender/windowmanager/WM_types.h* related to operators, as some represent different events, etc. Some of these are wmEvent, wmDrag, wmTimer, and wmKeyMap. We will address these types as they arise in our discussions about event handling.

The **exec** and **poll** Callbacks

You will find in the codebase comments brief descriptions of each "function" field of wmOperatorType. However, to simplify our discussion, we focus on only the two required callbacks: exec and poll.

The exec callback takes the bContext object as a parameter, and a wmOperator object, representing the handling for the associated event. The exec callback can leverage functionality from a given editor, which in turn may use one of the other Blender modules for even lower-level work.

As an example, let us look at the OUTLINER_OT_select_all() registration function (Listing 7-14). Note that we will cover the naming convention for operator registration functions in the next section.

Listing 7-14. The OUTLINER_OT_select_all() function is defined in source/blender/editors/space_outliner/outliner_edit.c. This operator is non-modal and only defines the minimum number of callbacks. We ignore the "RNA" component of the registration function

```
void OUTLINER_OT_select_all(wmOperatorType *ot)
{
  /* identifiers */
  ot->name = "Toggle Selected";
  ot->idname = "OUTLINER_OT_select_all";
  ot->description = "Toggle the Outliner selection of items";

  /* callbacks */
  ot->exec = outliner_select_all_exec;
  ot->poll = ED_operator_outliner_active;
  ...
}
```

This will be more clear in the next chapter when we create our own exec callback for an operator we create and register with our custom editor.

An event (e.g., a specific set of pressed keys) may be context dependent. The context is determined by the location of the mouse pointer in the application window and the mode that the application is in when an event occurs. We will see that the wmOperatorType provides a function for the windowmanager to call when handling events, which performs the needed work for checking the context via the bContext object (shown in Chapter 2).

Editors have been discussed, but the context is simply the state of the Blender application (e.g., "edit mode," "object mode," etc.). As an example, a mesh editing operation is not processed while in "object" mode, and only when the mouse pointer is over the "3D Viewport" editor.

Operator Registration

Operators are registered by editors and for the application window via the windowmanager module. Earlier in this chapter, we discussed editor registration.

As an example of operator registration in an editor, let us look at the function console_operatortypes(), the SpaceType.operatortypes value for the "console" editor. This function is shown in partial format in Listing 7-15.

Listing 7-15. The SpaceType.operatortypes field for the "console" editor. This function is defined in source/blender/editors/space_console/space_console.c. We see three of the operators for the "console" editor being registered here with the windowmanager

```
static void console_operatortypes(void)
{
  /* console_ops.c */
  WM_operatortype_append(CONSOLE_OT_move);
  WM_operatortype_append(CONSOLE_OT_delete);
  WM_operatortype_append(CONSOLE_OT_insert);

  ...
}
```

We notice that for each operator type specific to the "console" editor, it is registered with a function named CONSOLE_OT_*. We can see CONSOLE_OT_move in Listing 7-16.

Listing 7-16. The CONSOLE_OT_move operator type definition
function from source/blender/editors/space_console/console_
ops.c. In boldface is the idname field of wmOperatorType, which is the
key for the operator type lookup, during event handling, discussed
more in the next section

```
void CONSOLE_OT_move(wmOperatorType *ot)
{
  /* identifiers */
  ot->name = "Move Cursor";
  ot->description = "Move cursor position";
  ot->idname = "CONSOLE_OT_move";

  /* api callbacks */
  ot->exec = console_move_exec;
  ot->poll = ED_operator_console_active;

  /* properties */
  RNA_def_enum(
      ot->srna, "type", console_move_type_items, LINE_BEGIN,
      "Type", "Where to move cursor to");
}
```

There, the wmOperatorType is defined for this operator, and an idname
is assigned. This is the same char array as the identifier for the registration
function of the wmOperatorType.

The idname field will be used when inserting into the global_ops_hash
hash table from the function wm_operatortype_append__end(), seen
being called from WM_operatortype_append() in Listing 7-17.

Listing 7-17. `WM_operatortype_append()` from source/blender/
windowmanager/intern/wm_operator_type.c

```
void WM_operatortype_append(void (*opfunc)(wmOperatorType *))
{
  wmOperatorType *ot = wm_operatortype_append__begin();
  opfunc(ot);
  wm_operatortype_append__end(ot);
}
```

This is achieved in `wm_operatortype_append__end()` with a call to the blenlib module API: `BLI_ghash_insert(global_ops_hash, (void *) ot->idname, ot)`. The `global_ops_hash` variable is declared in *source/blender/windowmanager/intern/wm_operator_type.c*.

Naming Conventions

All of the operator type names start with either `WM_*` for `windowmanager` or the editor type, such as `CONSOLE_*`, `OUTLINER_*`, and so on. This is followed by `OT_*` and then information about the action and optionally additional information. Some examples for the `windowmanager` operators (i.e., operators that are handled at the Blender application window-level and not at the editor or region level) are

- `WM_OT_window_close`
- `WM_OT_window_new_main`
- `WM_OT_open_mainfile`

Event Distribution

You will recall from Chapter 1 that we discussed the main event loop in Listing 1-7. There, we saw that once the event loop `WM_main()` has been entered, the first function to be called at the top of the loop is `wm_window_process_events()`.

This function then calls GHOST_ProcessEvents(), to serve the available events via a call to ghost_event_proc(). The function ghost_event_proc() resides in the file *source/blender/windowmanager/intern/wm_window.c* and is partially shown in Listing 7-18. GHOST was covered in more detail in Chapter 3.

ghost_event_proc() handles events that are solely at the GHOST window-level. What is an event at the GHOST window-level? These events are anything not semantically Blender-specific, and therefore more general to an application's behavior. Examples are window resizing and application closing, among other application behaviors.

Let us look at how ghost_event_proc() treats the GHOST_kEventOpenMainFile event. Refer to Listing 7-18 once again. WM_operatortype_find() is used to look up a registered operator (an wmOperatorType object). In this example, the operator-type struct is accessed via the hashed char array "WM_OT_open_mainfile," from global_ops_hash—a GHash hash table.

GHash is implemented in *source/blender/blenlib/intern/BLI_ghash.c.* You will recall we covered the blenlib module in Chapter Four. BLI_* API functions are used to access and manipulate a GHash object. This particular data structure is used, as it is O(1) in search time on average. This is necessary, because of the timing requirements of handling events. Obviously, there is a trade-off for speed over storage.

Once the proper wmOperatorType object is found, Data API calls are made to prepare the relevant "RNA" properties data (with "display_file_selector"). Then these properties are passed to WM_operator_name_call_ptr(). There will need to be modal interaction with the file browser later. So, all that is being done here is opening a file browser editor. This process is similar to wm_event_do_handlers(), except for the event queues in the active wmWindow object.

Listing 7-18. Snippet from ghost_event_proc(), found in the file: source/blender/windowmanager/intern/wm_window.c. Calls either directly to an operator or added to the window's events queue (events to be handled) are shown for a few select events for illustration and thus shown in boldface

```
static int ghost_event_proc(GHOST_EventHandle evt, GHOST_
TUserDataPtr C_void_ptr)
{
  bContext *C = C_void_ptr;
  wmWindowManager *wm = CTX_wm_manager(C);
  GHOST_TEventType type = GHOST_GetEventType(evt);
  ...
  GHOST_WindowHandle ghostwin =  GHOST_GetEventWindow(evt);
  GHOST_TEventDataPtr data = GHOST_GetEventData(evt);
    wmWindow *win;
  ...
  win = GHOST_GetWindowUserData(ghostwin);
  ...
  switch (type) {
  ...
      case GHOST_kEventOpenMainFile: {
PointerRNA props_ptr;
        const char *path = GHOST_GetEventData(evt);

        if (path) {
          wmOperatorType *ot = WM_operatortype_find("WM_OT_
          open_mainfile", false);
          /* operator needs a valid window in context, ensures
           * it is correctly set */
          CTX_wm_window_set(C, win);

          WM_operator_properties_create_ptr(&props_ptr, ot);
```

```
            RNA_string_set(&props_ptr, "filepath", path);
            RNA_boolean_set(&props_ptr, "display_file_selector",
            false);
            WM_operator_name_call_ptr(C, ot, WM_OP_INVOKE_
            DEFAULT, &props_ptr);
            WM_operator_properties_free(&props_ptr);

            CTX_wm_window_set(C, NULL);
          }
          break;
        }
    ...
        case GHOST_kEventButtonDown:
        case GHOST_kEventButtonUp: {
    ...
          wm_event_add_ghostevent(wm, win, type, data);
          break;
        }
        default: {
          wm_event_add_ghostevent(wm, win, type, data);
          break;
        }
      }
    }
    return 1;
}
```

We can see in ghost_event_proc() that events which eventually
go on to be handled at lower levels (i.e., in "areas" or "regions") need to
go on the active window's event queue. For the shown events "GHOST_
KEventButtonDown" and "GHOST_KEventButtonUp," wm_event_add_
ghostevent() is called. These functional calls are highlighted in Listing 7-19.

The purpose of wm_event_add_ghostevent() is to process GHOST events, by further sorting and then adding information (mouse position, Blender keypress code, etc.) to a wmEvent object. The appropriately recorded wmEvent is then passed to the active wmWindow struct via wm_event_add(). An excerpt from wm_event_add_ghostevent() is provided in Listing 7-19.

Listing 7-19. Snippet from wm_add_ghostevent(), defined in source/blender/windowmanager/intern/wm_event_system.c. GHOST_kEventButtonDown and GHOST_kEventButtonUp are only representative, and many other event types—such as mouse movement and keypresses—are also processed via wm_add_ghostevent()

```
void wm_event_add_ghostevent(wmWindowManager *wm, wmWindow
*win, int type, void *customdata)
{
  ...
  wmEvent event, *evt = win->eventstate;
  ...
  event = *evt;

  switch (type) {
    ...
    /* mouse button */
    case GHOST_kEventButtonDown:
    case GHOST_kEventButtonUp: {
      GHOST_TEventButtonData *bd = customdata;

      /* get value and type from ghost */
      event.val = (type == GHOST_kEventButtonDown) ? KM_PRESS :
      KM_RELEASE;
```

```
    if (bd->button == GHOST_kButtonMaskLeft) {
      event.type = LEFTMOUSE;
    }
    ...
      wm_event_add(win, &event);
    ...
    break;
  }
  ...
 }
}
```

After wm_window_process_events() returns in WM_main(), wm_event_do_handlers() is called.[1] See Listing 7-20. In essence, the wm_event_do_handlers() does the following:

- Loops over all wmWindow objects (i.e., the Blender windows)

- Retrieves the active Scene and ViewLayer objects

- For each wmWindow object

  - Traverses its respective event queue

  - For each such event (a wmEvent object)

    - Finds the Editor region the event occured

    - And then, calls wm_handlers_do() passing the corresponding AreaRegion object

---

[1]Note that after wm_event_do_handlers() returns, wm_event_do_notifiers() is called in WM_main(). We do not cover notifiers here, as they are similar to events, and a further specification on events, used by Blender for efficiency in updating (drawing) the user interface.

Listing 7-20. Snippet from wm_event_do_handlers() in source/
blender/windowmanager/intern/wm_event_system.c. Note that
the macro ED_screen_areas_itr declares and initializes a ScrArea
pointer named sa. The key steps in the algorithm are in boldface

```
void wm_event_do_handlers(bContext *C)
{
  wmWindowManager *wm = CTX_wm_manager(C);
  wmWindow *win;
  ...
  for (win = wm->windows.first; win; win = win->next)
  {
    bScreen *screen = WM_window_get_active_screen(win);
    wmEvent *event;
  ...
    Main *bmain = CTX_data_main(C);
    Scene *scene = WM_window_get_active_scene(win);
    ViewLayer *view_layer = WM_window_get_active_view_
    layer(win);
  ...
    while ((event = win->queue.first)) {
      int action = WM_HANDLER_CONTINUE;
      ...
      if ((action & WM_HANDLER_BREAK) == 0) {
        ARegion *ar;
        ...
        ED_screen_areas_iter(win, screen, sa)
        {
          ...
          if (wm_event_inside_rect(event, &sa->totrct)) {
            CTX_wm_area_set(C, sa);
```

```
if ((action & WM_HANDLER_BREAK) == 0) {
    for (ar = sa->regionbase.first; ar; ar = ar->next) {
        if (wm_event_inside_region(event, ar)) {

            CTX_wm_region_set(C, ar);

            /* call even on non mouse events, since the */
            wm_region_mouse_co(C, event);
            ...

            action |= wm_handlers_do(C, event,
            &ar->handlers);
```
...

wm_handlers_do(), with further processing for multi-click events
(not shown), calls wm_handlers_do_internal(). In wm_handlers_
do_internal() calls the appropriate wm_handler_*_call(), which is
eventually responsible for calling the appropriate callback function in the
wmOperatorType. Also, during editor registration, the ARegion struct
is provided a list of wmEventHandler structs (implemented in *source/
blender/windowmanager/wm_event_system.h*), defining which event types
a region should process.

Summary

This chapter covered the editors module and the foundation of the
Blender operators implementation. We skipped over the concept of
notifiers—and even action zones—in order to focus on the operator and
event mechanism, by looking at non-modal operator registration and
event messaging (i.e., the distribution of events to the specific window,
area, or region handling the event).

As an exercise, find the code that allows Python operators to be defined, registered, and called by the Blender runtime. The operator callbacks are implemented in Python script, not compiled C code. The starting point is the source file: *source/blender/python/intern/bpy_operator_wrap.c*. See the material in Chapter 5, for more information on how Blender embeds the Python interpreter.

CHAPTER 8

Editor Creation

In this final chapter, we add a new editor to the Blender codebase. Doing so will help us to better understand editor implementation. It will also provide a platform for adding a simple button layout using Blender's custom user interface (UI) API. Along the way, we will encounter the gpu module, an abstraction layer for Blender's underlying hardware-based rendering API (i.e., OpenGL).[1] We will also register a few non-modal operators for our editor. All of this will be done directly in the codebase's C code.

Drawing Editors from WM_main()

Before we discuss using the structs such as SpaceType, ARegion, etc. for creating an editor from scratch, let us consider again the main event loop WM_main(), from *source/blender/windowmanager/intern/wm.c* (shown in Listing 1-7). You will recall we covered the SpaceType, ARegion, and ARegionType structs in the previous chapter. These structs will be referenced again in this chapter.

The last function call in this loop is wm_draw_update(). It is in this call, after Blender's data has been updated in the given loop, that we draw the ARegion "data-blocks" for each of our editors.

---

[1]A discussion of OpenGL is beyond the scope of this book. A standard resource for learning OpenGL is the "OpenGL Programming Guide," by Shreiner et al.

© Brad E. Hollister 2021
B. E. Hollister, *Core Blender Development*,
https://doi.org/10.1007/978-1-4842-6415-7_8

Note   Data-blocks are the member data portion (or "block of data") of an object in Blender. As Blender is written in C, and not afforded the class construction of C++, it breaks the notion of a class into two parts: the type and the data-block. Thus, for a region, we have the ARegionType, which must be initialized with the required functions for the type using function pointer assignment, and ARegion, the "data-block" portion which has a pointer to the type-part along with instance-specific data, such as the viewable area of a region stored in its View2D type field, called v2d. As we first saw in Chapter 5, when we talked about how derived types are defined in the CPython API, this pattern is similar and generally how C programs perform "subclassing" and object creation using structs.

Remember, Blender supports multiple windows as well, so within wm_draw_update(), we iterate over all of the windows and then their respective screens (the ScrArea data-block) down to each ARegion object in a wmWindow's hierarchy. You should refer back to earlier chapters for the relevant structs, if necessary. In Listing 8-1, we see a snippet from wm_draw_update().

Listing 8-1. Elided wm_draw_update() from source/blender/windowmanager/intern/wm_draw.c. Here, we iterate over each wmWindow struct, from the singleton wmWindowManager object. For each wmWindow object, a call is made to wm_draw_window(). Lines of interest are in boldface

```
void wm_draw_update(bContext *C)
{
  Main *bmain = CTX_data_main(C);
  wmWindowManager *wm = CTX_wm_manager(C);
```

```
wmWindow *win;
...
for(win = wm->windows.first; win; win = win->next){
...

    ...
    CTX_wm_window_set(C, win);
    ...
    wm_draw_window(C, win);
    ...
    wm_window_swap_buffers(win);
    ...
  }
}
```

In Listing 8-2, we show wm_draw_window(). Only regions tagged for redraw are copied from an offscreen buffer (i.e., "blitted" to video memory) to an eventual front-buffer, to be shown on the computer monitor. The original off-screen drawing is done in wm_draw_window_offscreen(). We ignore the special cases for stereo rendering (right and left separate views) to the visible buffer.

For the remainder of this section, we focus on the path of execution down to the editor's draw functions. Editor draw functions themselves will be covered in the **Adding a Custom Editor** section of this chapter.

Listing 8-2. Snippet from wm_draw_window() from source/blender/windowmanager/intern/wm_draw.c. Calls to wm_draw_window_offscreen() and wm_draw_window_onscreen() are shown in boldface

```
static void wm_draw_window(bContext *C, wmWindow *win)
{
  bScreen *screen = WM_window_get_active_screen(win);
  bool stereo = WM_stereo3d_enabled(win, false);
```

```
...
wm_draw_window_offscreen(C, win, stereo);

/* Now we draw into the window framebuffer, in full window
   coordinates. */
if (!stereo) {
  /* Regular mono drawing. */
  wm_draw_window_onscreen(C, win, -1);
}
...
screen->do_draw = false;
}
```

Next, we see `wm_draw_window_offscreen()`, in Listing 8-3. The lines of code dedicated to stereo view, menu drawing, etc. have been omitted. Note the eventual call to `ED_region_do_draw()` in the nested loop interior. Lines of current interest are in boldface. The `ED_screen_areas_iter` macro was discussed in Chapter 7.

Listing 8-3. `wm_draw_window_offscreen()` from source/blender/windowmanager/intern/wm_draw.c

```
static void wm_draw_window_offscreen(bContext *C, wmWindow
*win, bool stereo)
{
  Main *bmain = CTX_data_main(C);
  wmWindowManager *wm = CTX_wm_manager(C);
  bScreen *screen = WM_window_get_active_screen(win);

  /* Draw screen areas into own frame buffer. */
  ED_screen_areas_iter(win, screen, sa)
  {
    CTX_wm_area_set(C, sa);
```

```
/* Compute UI layouts for dynamically size regions. */
for (ARegion *ar = sa->regionbase.first; ar; ar = ar->next)
{

  ...
/* Then do actual drawing of regions. */
for (ARegion *ar = sa->regionbase.first; ar; ar = ar->next)
{
    if (ar->visible && ar->do_draw) {
      CTX_wm_region_set(C, ar);
      bool use_viewport = wm_region_use_viewport(sa, ar);
    ...
        wm_draw_region_buffer_create(ar, false, use_
        viewport);
        wm_draw_region_bind(ar, 0);
        ED_region_do_draw(C, ar);
        wm_draw_region_unbind(ar, 0);
      }

      ar->do_draw = false;
      CTX_wm_region_set(C, NULL);
    ...
  }
  ...
}
```

Finally, we look at ED_region_do_draw() in Listing 8-4. We have now reached the call to the registered function in the "data-block" ARegion.

This struct has an ARegionType member, representing its type-based attributes, such as function pointers. The one of concern here is draw, which points to a registered draw function for an editor's region. The call to a region's draw function is shown in boldface.

Listing 8-4. `ED_region_do_draw()` snippet from source/blender/
editors/screen/area.c

```
void ED_region_do_draw(bContext *C, ARegion *ar)
{
  wmWindow *win = CTX_wm_window(C);
  ScrArea *sa = CTX_wm_area(C);
  ARegionType *at = ar->type;
  ...

    at->draw(C, ar);
  ...
  /* XXX test: add convention to end regions always in pixel
    space,
   * for drawing of borders/gestures etc */
  ED_region_pixelspace(ar);

  ED_region_draw_cb_draw(C, ar, REGION_DRAW_POST_PIXEL);

  region_draw_azones(sa, ar);
  ...
  }
```

Adding a Custom Editor

In this section, we cover the basics of creating an editor within the Blender application. The Blender codebase does provide the ability to customize the existing editors, using Blender's extended and embedded Python interpreter. However, it is not possible to create new editors. In Figure 8-1, we can see this chapter's tutorial editor as a selection in the Editor menu.

Figure 8-1. *The "Tutorial Editor" selectable from the Editor Type menu*

We learned about the editors module in Chapter 7. Now, we add one of our own and outline the necessary files that need to be affected and the functions that a SpaceType needs to have defined.

The previous section led us to the draw function, which is one of the needed functions for the SpaceType struct, used in defining an editor. Our editor (shown in Figure 8-2) will consist of the following:

- It will have two separate regions:

  - The first is a header-type region.[2]

  - The second is a window-type region.[3]

- The header will contain three buttons, with text descriptions, all implemented in C.

---

[2]Note that the regular editors provided in the Blender codebase have their header regions defined in Python. Also, their headers have a menu which allows for selection of a different region from the one that is displayed.

[3]This should not be confused with a wmWindow object. This refers to a part of a Blender window's screen within an editor, instead. Recall Chapter 7's discussion of the divisions of Blender application windows.

- Each button will have its own operator, whose exec function will run when the button is clicked.

- The exec functions will set a background color of red, green, or blue. And, this color will be stored in the SpaceTutorial object associated with a given instance of the editor.

- The window region will have three rectangles drawn into it using the gpu module.

    - The dimensions of the rectangles are determined by the View2D struct from the ARegion object of the window region.

- The editor will be included in the makesrna module list, so that it is available to the Blender Python API. However, we will not provide the code necessary in any particular region for executing the register Python class' code to either register operators or draw UI elements.

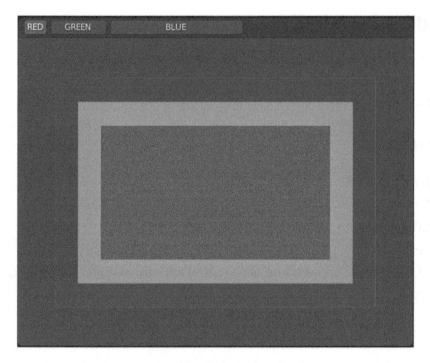

Figure 8-2. *The "Tutorial Editor." Three header buttons and the prominent* RGN_TYPE_WINDOW *main region*

Our editor, while minimal, illustrates

- How to define UI buttons[4] in an editor

- How to register operators and associate them with UI elements

- How to define separate regions within a SpaceType (i.e., editor)

- How to draw into a window region, using the gpu module's API

---

[4]IIn practice, it is better to implement such UI in the Python scripts that run at startup. This is more flexible and nearly as efficient, once registered and run from memory. However, using C in this chapter was intended as an introduction to the UI_*.

Editor Registration

Each editor is registered from the windowmanager module during WM_
init(). From WM_init(), ED_spacetypes_init() is called, which itself
then calls each of the editors' separate registration functions. Our tutorial
editor's registration function is ED_spacetype_tutorial(), and is shown
in Listing 8-5.

Listing 8-5. ED_spacetype_tutorial() from the new file: source/
blender/editors/space_tutorial/space_tutorial.c. A full list of
updated and additional files for the tutorial editor are given in a
later section. Note the enum value SPACE_TUTORIAL. This is defined
in DNA_space_types.h and is provided with the source code for this
chapter

```
void ED_spacetype_tutorial(void)
{
  SpaceType *st = MEM_callocN(sizeof(SpaceType), "spacetype
  tutorial");
  ARegionType *art;

  st->spaceid = SPACE_TUTORIAL;
  strncpy(st->name, "Tutorial", BKE_ST_MAXNAME);

  st->new = tutorial_new;
  st->operatortypes = tutorial_operatortypes;

  /* regions: main window */
  art = MEM_callocN(sizeof(ARegionType), "spacetype tutorial
  main region");
  art->regionid = RGN_TYPE_WINDOW;
  art->init = tutorial_main_region_init;
  art->draw = tutorial_main_region_draw;
```

```
BLI_addhead(&st->regiontypes, art);

/* regions: header */
art = MEM_callocN(sizeof(ARegionType), "spacetype tutorial
header region");
art->regionid = RGN_TYPE_HEADER;
art->prefsizey = HEADERY;
art->keymapflag = ED_KEYMAP_UI | ED_KEYMAP_VIEW2D |
ED_KEYMAP_HEADER;
art->init = tutorial_header_region_init;
art->draw = tutorial_header_region_draw;
art->prefsizey = HEADERY;

BLI_addhead(&st->regiontypes, art);

BKE_spacetype_register(st);
}
```

We must allocate memory through the intern library guardedalloc, the
Blender memory management API discussed in Chapter 1. We first do this
for the SpaceType. We also assign two function pointers for the SpaceType,
init and operatortypes. These functions will be discussed soon.

In ED_spacetype_tutorial(), two regions are defined for the editor
and then added to the editor's SpaceType. The blendlib module's
API function BLI_addhead() is used to append the region types to the
SpaceType's regiontypes ListBase field. In essence, adding each to the
front of the linked list of region types.

Each region's type is specified by filling out its corresponding
ARegionType object, each allocated using MEM_callocN(). There are many
fields in the ARegionType struct. As a minimum, we set the init and
draw function pointers.

The SpaceType's new Function

The new function pointer's type definition for SpaceType is shown in Listing 8-6. Of note, this function returns a pointer to a heap-allocated SpaceLink type (Listing 8-7) object, which represents the data portion of an editor.

Listing 8-6. The new function pointer type from the SpaceType struct in source/blender/blenkernel/BKE_screen.h. A comment is included, as it describes the new function's purpose in editor instantiation. The new function type's definition is in boldface

```
/* Initial allocation, after this WM will call init() too. Some
   editors need
   * area and scene data (e.g. frame range) to set their
     initial scrolling. */

  struct SpaceLink *(*create)(const struct ScrArea *sa, const
  struct Scene *scene);
```

Listing 8-7. The SpaceLink "base" struct from source/blender/makesdna/DNA_space_types.h

```
/**
 * The base structure all the other spaces
 * are derived (implicitly) from. Would be
 * good to make this explicit.
 */
typedef struct SpaceLink {
  struct SpaceLink *next, *prev;
  /** Storage of regions for inactive spaces. */
  ListBase regionbase;
  char spacetype;
  char link_flag;
```

```
char _pad0[6];
} SpaceLink;
```

In our tutorial, we forgo the init function to keep things simple. However, we must define a "derived" type from SpaceLink.

Our tutorial editor's SpaceLink is called SpaceTutorial (shown in Listing 8-8). As we want to store the background color of the editor's main region, we provide the color field. The color field is of type int and is assigned a proper enum value from *source/blender/editors/space_tutorial/ space_tutorial.c*.

We will see that our button operators set the color field in a SpaceTutorial object. If we had included an init function for our editor's SpaceType, then we may have initialized the color field there. Instead, we simply have a default case in our operators' exec function.

Listing 8-8. Our SpaceTutorial struct, added to source/blender/ makesdna/DNA_space_types.h. The color field is in boldface

```
/* SpaceTutorial */
typedef struct SpaceTutorial {
  SpaceLink *next, *prev;
  /** Storage of regions for inactive spaces. */
  ListBase regionbase;
  char spacetype;
  int color;
  char _pad0[6];
  /* End 'SpaceLink' header. */
} SpaceTutorial;
```

tutorial_new() is the function we assign to SpaceType's new field. It is shown in Listing 8-9. As already stated, it is the function that is called when a new instance of our editor is created by the user. The data portions of not only the SpaceType (i.e., the SpaceTutorial SpaceLink object) but the editor's regions—its ARegion objects—are also allocated and initialized.

Note that the spacetype field of the SpaceLink (i.e., SpaceTutorial) is assigned the enum value SPACE_TUTORIAL, just as the editor's SpaceType's spaceid field was. Similarly, the ARegions objects have their regiontype fields assigned to the same value as the editor's corresponding ARegionTypes' regionid fields. In this case, we have RGN_TYPE_HEADER assigned to the header's ARegion object, and RGN_TYPE_WINDOW assigned to the main region's ARegion object.

Listing 8-9. The tutorial_new() function from our new file source/ blender/editors/space_tutorial/space_tutorial.c. The assignment of the spacetype field is in boldface. Notice that neither area or scene, while both parts of the required function type for SpaceType's new field, are used in this implementation. There is an UNUSED macro that we introduce later, to mark such cases

```
static SpaceLink *tutorial_new(const ScrArea * area, const
Scene* scene)
{
  ARegion *ar;
  SpaceTutorial *stut;

  stut = MEM_callocN(sizeof(*stut), "new tutorial");
  stut->spacetype = SPACE_TUTORIAL;

  /* header */
  ar = MEM_callocN(sizeof(ARegion), "header for tutorial");

  BLI_addtail(&stut->regionbase, ar);
  ar->regiontype = RGN_TYPE_HEADER;
  ar->alignment = RGN_ALIGN_BOTTOM;

  /* main region */
  ar = MEM_callocN(sizeof(ARegion), "main region of tutorial");
```

```
BLI_addtail(&stut->regionbase, ar);
ar->regiontype = RGN_TYPE_WINDOW;

return (SpaceLink *)stut;
}
```

Editor Regions

As we just saw, our editor contains two regions, a header and window (main region), and that there are two ARegionType structs for those regions—both defined in tutorial_new(). Here, we look at the function definitions in the ARegionTypes for draw and init, which were assigned earlier in ED_spacetype_tutorial().

The **ARegionTypes' init** Functions

The regions' init functions work similar to the editor top-level init function. Now, however, we must handle any specific lower-level initialization for the given region.

As there are many standard procedures for initializing headers in editors, we simply call the ED_region_header_init() API function in tutorial_header_region_init(). This can be seen in Listing 8-10.

Listing 8-10. The tutorial_header_region_init() function. As we are not using the wmWindowManager parameter of the function type's specification, we mark this parameter with the UNUSED macro. This is optional, but considered good practice

```
static void tutorial_header_region_init(wmWindowManager
*UNUSED(wm), ARegion *ar)
{
  ED_region_header_init(ar);
}
```

In Listing 8-11, we show `tutorial_main_region_init()`. We will be drawing into the main region using its `ARegion`'s `View2D` struct field. Therefore, we call `UI_view2d_region_reinit()`.

Listing 8-11. The `tutorial_main_region_init()` function

```
static void tutorial_main_region_init(wmWindowManager
*UNUSED(wm), ARegion *region)
{
  UI_view2d_region_reinit(&region->v2d, V2D_COMMONVIEW_CUSTOM,
  region->winx, region->winy);
}
```

The Main Region's **draw** Function

Listing 8-12 shows the `tutorial_main_region_draw()` function definition. We will talk more about the header region draw function later, when we address button creation. For now, consider `tutorial_main_region_draw()`.

The first thing we do in `tutorial_main_region_draw()` is to gain access to the `SpaceTutorial` (data-block for our editor), from the context, using `CTX_wm_space_tutorial()`.

Listing 8-12. The `tutorial_main_region_draw()` function. In the section of the function, where we draw concentric rectangles, the offsets between rectangles are given specific values as opposed to scaling with the height and width of the main region's extents[5]

```
static void tutorial_main_region_draw(const bContext *C,
ARegion *ar)
{
```

---

[5]An improved version of `tutorial_main_region_draw()` might use scaled offsets when the editor's extents are smaller than the hard-coded ones. However, this would complicate the code and potentially obscure the purpose of exposing the basic mechanics of editor creation.

```
SpaceTutorial* stut = CTX_wm_space_tutorial(C);
View2D *v2d = &ar->v2d;

switch(stut->color){
    case GREEN:
      GPU_clear_color(0.0, 1.0, 0.0, 1.0);
      break;
    case BLUE:
      GPU_clear_color(0.0, 0.0, 1.0, 1.0);
      break;
    case RED:
    default:
      GPU_clear_color(1.0, 0.0, 0.0, 1.0);
  }

GPU_clear(GPU_COLOR_BIT);

/* draw colored rectangles within mask area of region */

uint pos = GPU_vertformat_attr_add(
  immVertexFormat(), "pos", GPU_COMP_I32, 2, GPU_FETCH_INT_
  TO_FLOAT);
immBindBuiltinProgram(GPU_SHADER_2D_UNIFORM_COLOR);

immUniformColor4ub(255, 0, 255, 255);
immRecti(pos,
        v2d->mask.xmin + 50,
        v2d->mask.ymin + 50,
        v2d->mask.xmax - 50,
        v2d->mask.ymax - 50);
```

```
immUniformColor4ub(0, 255, 255, 255);
immRecti(pos,
         v2d->mask.xmin + 80,
         v2d->mask.ymin + 80,
         v2d->mask.xmax - 80,
         v2d->mask.ymax - 80);

immUniformColor4ub(255, 255, 0, 255);
immRecti(pos,
         v2d->mask.xmin + 110,
         v2d->mask.ymin + 110,
         v2d->mask.xmax - 110,
         v2d->mask.ymax - 110);

immUnbindProgram();
}
```

Our implementation of CTX_wm_space_tutorial() is added to *source/blender/blenkernel/intern/context.c* and can be found in the source code provided for this chapter. Its purpose is to return the corresponding SpaceLink for the editor instance from the context. In addition to the editor's data-block, we also make sure to obtain a pointer to the ARegion's View2D, from the editor's window-type region. This will allow us to use its mask field, that is, the drawing surface of the main region.

Subsequent to obtaining the needed pointers, we set the background color using the gpu module's GPU_clear_color (). While this could have been done with a direct call to OpenGL, it is a better practice to use the gpu module's wrapper for this. We also make a call to GPU_clear(GPU_COLOR_BIT) to actually clear the buffer.

The remainder of tutorial_main_region_draw() draws the concentric rectangles. Interesting, the gpu module still supports an immediate mode interface to OpenGL. Thus, the code for drawing the concentric rectangles resembles an obsolescent method relative to current versions of OpenGL. The earlier Blender codebase, however, often used immediate mode for drawing. The gpu module's immediate mode interface (functions prefaced with imm*) has kept much of the codebase's drawing code similar to its original form.

Operator Registration and Definition

Our operator definitions and registration are straightforward and follow the material from Chapter 7, where we talked about WM_operatortype_append() and wmOperatorType.

We first inspect the operators registered for our editor, in Listing 8-13, via tutorial_operatortypes(). It should be noted that tutorial_operatortypes() has already been assigned to our editor's SpaceType's operatortypes field, in ED_spacetype_tutorial().

Listing 8-13. The tutorial_operatortypes() function

```
void tutorial_operatortypes(void)
{
  WM_operatortype_append(
    SPACE_TUTORIAL_OT_red_region);
  WM_operatortype_append(
    SPACE_TUTORIAL_OT_green_region);
  WM_operatortype_append(
    SPACE_TUTORIAL_OT_blue_region);
}
```

Calls to WM_operatortype_append() are passed our operator registration functions. We assign three separate, but very similar, operators for each button in our editor's header. Button rendering will be discussed in the next section.

We show one of our operator registration functions, SPACE_TUTORIAL_OT_red_region() in Listing 8-14. Here, the operators are all non-modal.

Only the required exec and poll function pointers are assigned in each of the SPACE_TUTORIAL_OT_*_region() functions.

Listing 8-14. The SPACE_TUTORIAL_OT_red_region() function

```
void SPACE_TUTORIAL_OT_red_region(wmOperatorType *ot)
{
  /* identifiers */
  ot->name = "Red Region Button";
  ot->description = "Turns the main region background to red";
  ot->idname = "SPACE_TUTORIAL_OT_red_region";

  /* api callbacks */
  ot->exec = set_background_red_in_main_region;
  ot->poll = test_context_for_button_operator;

  /* flags */
  ot->flag = OPTYPE_REGISTER;
}
```

As our tutorial editor is meant to be as simple as possible—such that the context or mode does not affect the operator's function—the poll callback test_context_for_button_operator returns non-zero (i.e., "true") for all calls.

The exec callback, set_background_red_in_main_region(), works by setting the proper enum value in the editor's data-block color field—that is, a particular instance's SpaceTutorial object. This can be seen in Listing 8-15.

Listing 8-15. The set_background_red_in_main_region() function

```
int set_background_red_in_main_region(struct bContext *C,
struct wmOperator *oper) {
```

```
    SpaceTutorial* stut = CTX_wm_space_tutorial(C);
    ARegion *ar = CTX_wm_region(C);

  stut->color = 1;

  ED_area_tag_redraw(CTX_wm_area(C));

  return OPERATOR_FINISHED;
}
```

Each of the operator exec functions does the same, for their respective background color.

Header Buttons

The UI_* API is rather extensive. Blender "RNA" wraps it, for the Blender Python API, as much of the UI is scripted in Python. However, for illustration purposes, we use the UI_* API directly in our editor.

From the draw function of our header region, we call draw_our_GUI_ in_C(). This function's partial implementation is shown in Listing 8-16.

Listing 8-16. The partial implementation of draw_our_buttons_ in_C(). The lines of code related to assigning a button's operator type are in boldface. Note that this is done every time the header region is redrawn

```
static void draw_our_buttons_in_C(uiBlock* block) {

  struct wmOperatorType* ot = WM_operatortype_find("SPACE_
  TUTORIAL_OT_red_region", true);

  struct uiBut* but = uiDefBut(block, // uiBlock*
    UI_BTYPE_BUT_TOGGLE,  // int type
    1,                    // int retval
```

```
        "RED",                  // const char *str
        100,                    // int x1
        2,                      // int y1
        30,                     // short x2
        19,                     // short y2
        NULL,                   // void *poin to char...
        0.0,                    // float min
        0.0,                    // float max
        0.0,                    // float a1
        0.0,                    // float a2
        "");                    // const char *tip

    but->optype = ot;

    ...
```

Every time `tutorial_header_region_draw()` is executed, so is `draw_our_buttons_in_C()`. In `draw_our_buttons_in_C()`, we call `uiDefBut()`. The `uiDefBut()` function is passed a `uiBlock struct`, which is the grouping for our header buttons. It is used for coordination purposes (i.e., a "block" of buttons may be radial, in that only one of the group can be selected at any one time).

Our buttons do not retain a state after being clicked, so we use the toggle type identified by the `UI_BTYPE_BUT_TOGGLE` enum value. The button shown in Listing 8-16 is for the button that when clicked, sets the background color of our editor's window (main) region to red. We therefore use a text label on the button, as can be seen in the actual parameters. The remaining parameters are used for setting the placement and size of a button in the region's coordinate system, which starts in the lower left of the region. We will talk more about the `UI_*` API itself in an upcoming section of this chapter.

Importantly, we use the returned pointer to a `uiBut` object, to set the button's operator type. In the very first line of `draw_our_GUI_in_C()`, we called WM_operatortype_find(). The idname field we set in SPACE_ TUTORIAL_OT_red_region() is passed. WM_operatortype_find() returns the wmOperatorType from the SPACE_TUTORIAL_OT_red_region() registration. We have the operator type from the outset of draw_our_GUI_in_C(), allowing us to set the optype of the returned uiBut object. This connects the clicking event of the button to the operator. When the button is clicked, the poll callback is first called, then the exec callback, of the operator.

File Changes for the Tutorial Editor

The entirety of additional files and changes can be found in the source code included with this book. Tables 8-1, 8-2, and 8-3 summarize the files added or affected.

Table 8-1. *Summary of source files.*
Boldface files are new

Source File
source/blender/blenkernel/intern/context.c
source/blender/editors/space_api/spacetypes.c
source/blender/editors/space_tutorial/space_tutorial.c
source/blender/makesrna/intern/rna_space.c

Completely new files are *space_tutorial.c* and *space_tutorial.h*, as seen in Tables 8-1 and 8-2, respectively. These source files contain code that was not covered in the previous section **Editor Registration**. You may choose to split up the code in space_tutorial.c into separate source files, as many of the editors do this. As the tutorial editor is rather short, this approach was not taken here. Often, the operators occupy a source file of their own, and each of the regions also has its own source and header files.

One thing to be aware of is that without updating *rna_space.c* or *RNA_access.h,* your editor will not be available to the Blender Python API. If you fail to update these two files, the editor type used in scripted UI will fail to find the new editor.

Table 8-2. *Summary of header files. Boldface files are new*

Header File
source/blender/blenkernel/BKE_context.h
source/blender/editors/include/ED_space_api.h
source/blender/makesdna/DNA_space_types.h
source/blender/makesrna/RNA_access.h

Table 8-3. *Summary of build files. Boldface files are new*

Build Script
source/blender/editors/CMakeLists.txt
source/blender/editors/space_tutorial/CMakeLists.txt
source/blender/makesrna/intern/CMakeLists.txt

The User Interface API

There is official documentation on the UI_* API. It resides in *doc/guides/interface_API.txt.*

While this document is helpful, it is out-of-date.[6] That said, it still provides insight on the origin and workings of the Blender UI system. Thus, *interface_API.txt* should be considered first, before using the API.

Headers

The user interface API implementation files (UI_*) are located in *source/blender/editors/interface/*. The UI_* API prototypes, however, are located in *source/blender/editors/include/*. The dependency graph for this directory is shown in Figure 8-3.

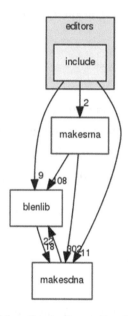

Figure 8-3. *The source/blender/editors/include/ dependency graph. Since access to structs such as View2D is provided from UI_view2d.h, and other files in this directory, there are many connections with the* makesdna *module*

---

[6]The path and file information in *doc/guides/interface_API.txt* is incorrect and should be read with caution. There are also enums and earlier variants of functions that are no longer in the codebase.

There are five files that provide the UI_* API's prototypes to be used externally[7]—that is, for client code outside of *source/blender/editors/interface/*. The UI_* API's headers are

- UI_interface.h

- UI_view2d.h

- UI_resources.h

- UI_icons.h

- UI_interface_icons.h

UI_interface.h, *UI_view2d.h*, and *UI_resources.h* are used in the tutorial editor from this chapter.

UI_interface.h

The *UI_interface.h* file declares a number of API functions and enumerations for use in the codebase. A partial listing is shown in Listing 8-17. These functions are ones for creating (i.e., drawing at a high level) GUI elements and creating layouts. It is the longest and most extensive of the headers files.

---

[7]You will recall that we used the *source/blender/editors/interface/interface_intern.h* in our tutorial editor. This was to gain access to the struct uiBut, allowing us to manually assign its optype field with the wmOperatorType. Normally, you will be adding buttons via the Blender Python API, so including *interface_intern.h* in your editor's source file is neither necessary or advised—in order to maintain the preferred practice of encapsulation. The Blender codebase enforces this by not placing the implementation of the struct uiBut in the UI_*.h files. When code tries to access the struct uiBut outside of *editors/interface/*, while not using *interface_intern.h*, a "dereferencing pointer to incomplete type" compile error results.

Listing 8-17. Snippet of enums and prototypes from UI_interface.h

```
...
enum {
  UI_ID_RENAME = 1 << 0,
  UI_ID_BROWSE = 1 << 1,
  ...
};
...
uiBut *uiDefPulldownBut(...);
uiBut *uiDefMenuBut(...); ...
uiBut *uiDefBlockBut(...);
uiBut *uiDefBlockButN(...);
...
```

UI_view2d.h

This header gives access to the View2D struct, which is used for drawing on two-dimensional surfaces in editor regions. We saw an example of its use in our tutorial editor. Some of its function prototypes are shown in Listing 8-18.

Listing 8-18. Example prototypes from UI_View2D.h

```
...
void UI_view2d_draw_lines_y__values(const struct View2D *v2d);
void UI_view2d_draw_lines_x__values(const struct View2D *v2d);
void UI_view2d_draw_lines_x__discrete_values(const struct
View2D *v2d ...);
...
```

UI_resources.h

"UI resources" are collectively related to theming and color schemes in the Blender UI. As such, enums for color and theme identification are defined in *UI_resources.h*, as are prototyped functions for getting and setting "UI resources." Listing 8-19 provides an example from this header file.

Listing 8-19. Snippet from UI_resources.h

```
...
void UI_GetThemeColorShade3fv(...);
void UI_GetThemeColorShade3ubv(...);
void UI_GetThemeColorShade4ubv(...);
...
```

While we do not cover the use of icons in the UI_* API, *UI_icons.h* and *UI_interface_icons.h* deal with this aspect of the Blender interface.

The UI_* API Implementation Files

Let us look at the directory layout in *source/blender/editors/interface/*, where the Blender UI_* API implementation resides (see Figure 8-4). There, we can see a number of files.

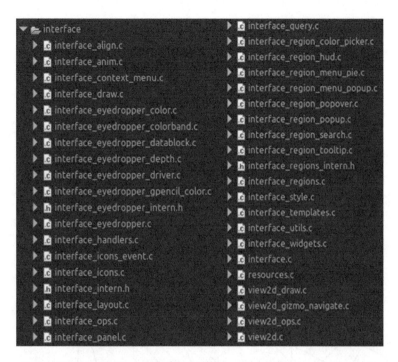

Figure 8-4. *The interface UI_* * API from the editors module, located at source/blender/editors/interface/*

These files are separated into ones that deal either with a particular category of UI elements, their operators, their handlers (callbacks from the operators), UI `structs` and `enum` definitions, or `View2D struct` functionality. The gpu module's API is called extensively by the UI interface code from this directory. This can be seen graphically in Figure 8-5.

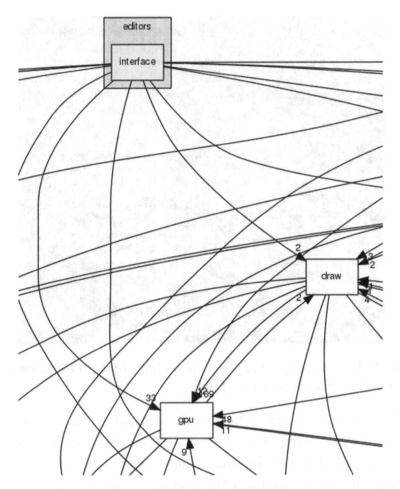

Figure 8-5. *Directory dependency graph for source/blender/editors/ interface/. Note the large number of references (total of thirty-three) to the gpu module*

Summary

If you are familiar with the Blender Python API, you will know that UI elements can be added via Python scripts. You will also be aware that operators can be registered via Python, and the python module will use the callbacks defined in Python scripts for the operator's functionality.

In this chapter, we did everything in C—the language of the "core" codebase. It will be instructive to go back to the tutorial editor, after completing the material in this chapter. Try to substitute the buttons and operator implementation, by instead using the Blender Python API. It should also be useful to trace the drawing of the editor, for cases when UI is implemented using the Blender Python API. The fundamentals of Blender's embedded Python interpreter were covered in Chapter 5 and are helpful in performing this exercise, along with knowledge of the "RNA" Data API[8] discussed in Chapter 6.

While the editor in this chapter was simple in function, it illustrated much of the logistics of editor implementation. Using the gpu module's drawing facilities, along with access to the Blender "DNA," a more realistic editor can be written. Use an editor like the "outliner" (*source/blender/editors/space_outliner/*) to see how this is done in practice.

As mentioned at the beginning of this book, there are still many topics in the Blender codebase left to explore. This book has provided the impetus and foundation for further Blender development. If you want to explore mesh modeling functionality, the code in *source/blender/editors/mesh* and the bmesh module are the places to begin. Or, perhaps you are interested in Blender's image processing capabilities. Thus, you should begin to look at the `compositor` module. These are just two of the many options to pursue.

---

[8]Hint: look into [repository directory]/*source/blender/makesrna/intern/rna_ui_api.c* and *rna_ui.c.* These implement the "RNA" Data API interface to the UI_* API.

Index

© Brad E. Hollister 2021
B. E. Hollister, *Core Blender Development*,
https://doi.org/10.1007/978-1-4842-6415-7

Printed in the United States
By Bookmasters